Woman
of Warfare

JOAN HARMON

WESTBOW
PRESS
A DIVISION OF THOMAS NELSON

WestBow Press books may be ordered through booksellers or by contacting:

WestBow Press
A Division of Thomas Nelson
1663 Liberty Drive
Bloomington, IN 47403
www.westbowpress.com
1-(866) 928-1240

Because of the dynamic nature of the Internet, any Web addresses or
links contained in this book may have changed since publication and
may no longer be valid. The views expressed in this work are solely those
of the author and do not necessarily reflect the views of the publisher,
and the publisher hereby disclaims any responsibility for them.

ISBN: 978-1-4497-0413-1 (sc)
ISBN: 978-1-4497-0578-7 (e)

Library of Congress Control Number: 2010935770

Printed in the United States of America

WestBow Press rev. date: 11/16/2011

TABLE OF CONTENTS

Opener

"For the Lord is faithful, He will make you strong and guard you from satanic attacks of every kind." 2 Thessalonians 3:3 (LVG)

Now you have done it, in confessing Christ as your Savior you have committed treason and the penalty for treason many times results in death. Or maybe you are considered A.W.O.L. and the enemy has sent his guard to bring you back. Or maybe you are seeking asylum from the strongholds that have been a part of your life for so long and you have come to the Embassy of Christ Jesus to escape the demons of your past and to start a new life in Christ. Well, congratulations are in order, because Jesus is now your "safe place" and He is loving and kind and He will guard and protect you.

Psalm 91:1-16 KJV

[1]He that dwelleth in the secret place of the most High shall abide under the shadow of the Almighty. [2]I will say of the LORD, He is my refuge and my fortress: my God; in him will I trust. [3]Surely he shall deliver thee from the snare of the fowler, and from the noisome pestilence. [4]He shall cover thee with his feathers, and under his wings shalt thou trust: his truth shall be thy shield and buckler. [5]Thou shalt not be afraid for the terror by night; nor for the arrow that flieth by day; [6]Nor for the pestilence that walketh in darkness; nor for the destruction that wasteth at noonday.

7A thousand shall fall at thy side, and ten thousand at thy right hand; but it shall not come nigh thee. 8Only with thine eyes shalt thou behold and see the reward of the wicked. 9Because thou hast made the LORD, which is my refuge, even the most High, thy habitation; 10There shall no evil befall thee, neither shall any plague come nigh thy dwelling.11For he shall give his angels charge over thee, to keep thee in all thy ways. 12They shall bear thee up in their hands, lest thou dash thy foot against a stone. 13Thou shalt tread upon the lion and adder: the young lion and the dragon shalt thou trample under feet. 14Because he hath set his love upon me, therefore will I deliver him: I will set him on high, because he hath known my name. 15He shall call upon me, and I will answer him: I will be with him in trouble; I will deliver him, and honour him. 16With long life will I satisfy him, and shew him my salvation.

You are now in the Lord's army! Remember that old army song: "You're in the army now." Well we sang one in Sunday school when I was a little girl and it goes like this:

"I may never march in the Infantry,
Ride in the cavalry, Shoot the artillery.
I may never fly o'er the enemy,
But I'm in the Lord's Army. I'm in the Lord's Army, …"

I remember singing that for years and going through the motions of it all but never really thought about it. It was a fun song to sing as a child. I'm thinking maybe we should have saved that one for the adult song service.

Many adults are very uncomfortable with the fact of being in the Lord's army, but it is a fact and we are soldiers whether we want to be or not. A very real war in the spirit surrounds us and we better be ready at all times to combat the forces of darkness. God has an army and if you are his child <u>you are in it!</u>

Ephesians 6:12-18 KJV

12For we wrestle not against flesh and blood, but against principalities, against powers, against the rulers of the darkness of this world, against spiritual wickedness in high places. [13]*Wherefore take unto you the whole armour of God, that ye may be able to withstand in the evil day, and having done all, to stand.* [14]*Stand therefore, having your loins girt about with truth, and having on the breastplate of righteousness;* [15]*And your feet shod with the preparation of the gospel of peace;* [16]*Above all, taking the shield of faith, wherewith ye shall be able to quench all the fiery darts of the wicked.* [17]*And take the helmet of salvation, and the sword of the Spirit, which is the word of God:* [18]*Praying always with all prayer and supplication in the Spirit, and watching thereunto with all perseverance and supplication for all saints;*

Isaiah 28:9-10

Whom shall he teach knowledge? And whom shall he make to understand doctrine? Them that are weaned from the milk and drawn from the breast. For precept must be upon precept, line upon line, line upon line, here a little, and there a little.

Chapter 1

ARMED AND DANGEROUS

Ephesians 6:10-18

10) Last of all I want to remind you that <u>your strength</u> must come from <u>the Lord's mighty power within you.</u> 11) Put on all of God's armor so that you will be able to stand <u>safe against all strategies</u> and "tricks" of Satan. 12) For we are not fighting against people made of flesh and blood but against person's without bodies - the evil rulers of the <u>unseen world,</u> those <u>mighty satanic</u> beings and great evil princes of darkness who <u>rule this world</u> and against huge numbers of wicked spirits in the spirit world. 13) So, <u>use every piece of God's armor</u> to resist the enemy whenever he attacks, and <u>when it is all over, you will be standing up!</u> 14) <u>BUT TO DO THIS,</u> you will need the <u>strong belt</u> of truth and the breastplate of God's approval. 15) Wear shoes <u>that are able to speed</u> you on as you preach the Good News of peace <u>with</u> God. 16) <u>In every battle</u> you will need faith as your shield to stop the fiery arrows aimed at you by Satan. 17) And you will need the helmet of salvation and the sword of the Spirit - which is the word of God. 18) Pray all the time...

*A*t this juncture in time, the Apostle Paul is addressing the Christians at Ephesus. The Christians at Ephesus were well aware of what they were up against in the spirit realm, after all, the city was a center of spiritualism. Ephesus was the city where the Temple of Diana dwelled and the inhabitants in the city were very familiar with demonic power. Ephesus swarmed with soothsayers and magicians and was the hub of all commerce. Talisman, charms and the like were used to ward off evil spirits as well as the use of incantations, rituals, and astrology. It was a city of witchcraft and many had come out of that lifestyle and were now Christians. In fact all through the book of Ephesians Paul is using their lingo to draw them to the one true God. And don't you know, being that Satan is our foe and does not give up his followers easily that the war was on. When those who were once his have now turned to Jesus Christ, one would expect nothing less. After all, he is a thief that cometh to steal, kill, and destroy. [John 10:10]

Even knowing this it is so sad to see in the church today how many are not taught upon their salvation experience how to stand against the enemy when he attacks and many succumb to the pressure of those anti-Christ spirits when they explode full throttle upon these innocent lambs. We need some armed and dangerous men and women of God who will teach and equip the saints for the battle of their souls after the victory of salvation, who in turn will themselves become armed and dangerous.

This to me seems logical because now you are considered a person of treason. You have left one camp and gone into the other. If we as men and women struggle with those who were once our friends but now seem to be so far away and aloof, how or why do we think, that Satan so evil in his ways and ruthless in his tactics would stand idly by and tip his hat when one leaves his fold and enters now into the fold of Jesus Christ. Most Christians sadly today do not even understand warfare, putting on the full armor and why all of that is necessary, after all Jesus has power over all power of the enemy right?

Colossians 2:10 KVJ

[10] *And ye are complete in him, which is the head of **all** principality and power:*

Well, let's put it this way. As a child your parent is not always around, once you hit the kindergarten circuit. Your parent has authority over you but even a little child has to stand on their own two feet when confronted with an adversary even of the same age. Even a child realizes they can run to a parent or authority figure for help and the parent will handle the situation properly and effectively, as they should. But as the child grows he is equipped more and more through life experiences and training to handle situations without running to the parent for help every time. Not that the parent couldn't handle it but there is a point where we should be able to rectify the situation knowing what to do. A forty year old man or woman is not going to call their parent to help them with a "bully" at work. By now you should be in a place as a "mature" adult to handle the situation. Remember: The church is for the equipping of the saints.

Ephesians 4:12 (LVG)

Why is it that he gives us these special abilities to do certain things best? It is that God's people will be equipped to do better work for him, building up the church, the body of Christ, to a position of strength and maturity.

So many want to take the passive way out and say, "Just leave it in the Lord's hands." Ephesians 4:4 We are all parts of the body... Christ is the head. Well, to that I say, "Who are the Lord's hands?" Are we not called parts of the Body of Christ? Are we not his instruments and administrators of his purposes? We walk with Jesus by our side at all times. He tells us in the word that he will never leave us or forsake us so He's there regardless of how you feel.

2 Corinthians 5:7

For we walk by faith, not by sight.

Paul is telling the Ephesians that God's mighty power is within them. To put on the full armor, they don't have to call on a demonic source anymore or use a charm of talisman with a "familiar" attached to it to protect them from other evil spirits, spirits of disease and sickness, spirits of lack and poverty, those "wicked spirits" in huge numbers with unseen bodies that are in league with Satan to bring destruction to mankind.

You know after being used in deliverance ministry for over 23 years I have seen a lot. I worked with a young woman for over 5 ½ years who had come out of a satanic cult in south Texas. We dealt with these very same issues after she gave her heart to Jesus.

When the demons would come to torment her and attack her after she came from Satan's camp into the Lord's her tendency would be to want to fight the enemy like she did when she served in the world of darkness. It was all she knew and she was not yet familiar with faith and trust in Jesus and she was just learning to wield her sword, which did not come easy. I remember even when she accepted Christ Jesus into her heart it was a month or so before she could even touch a bible let alone look at one. I remember what a great day it was when she called and told me that she had uncovered the bible I gave her and she could now look it. And then the day she could touch the bible that was a phenomenal day. And then when she was able to actually read scripture it was a glorious day!

Oh, you may shake your head but until you have been there and experienced this one really begins to understand what the Ephesians who came to Jesus must have dealt with upon their conversions. I'm sure the depth of darkness in their souls played a part in what they could handle to begin with and the continuing process of deliverance in their lives.

Paul was armed and dangerous. He sat at the feet of Gamaliel, one of the greatest rabbinical teachers of his time. Witchcraft was all over the known world and in practice during his day. Idolatry was everywhere and Paul was armed for this task of warfare in Ephesus. He would not have dared to go in and do what he did without the power of God working within Him to overcome the great evil deception in the lives of the Ephesians in this city. And many hated him. Why, because everything he stood for went against everything they believed in. And the "city" revolved around the worship of Diana! The world will hate you for you are one who has been crucified with Christ and it is no longer you that lives but Christ that lives within you.

John 15:18 KJV

If the world hate you, ye know that it hated me before it hated you.

In fact, there was an episode concerning Paul where for 2 hours the Ephesians shouted him down with "Great is Dianna of Ephesus." You cannot tell me that this was not a volatile situation that could of turned deadly for Paul.

Acts 19:23-34 (LVG)

23) And the same time there arose no small stir about that way. 24) For a certain man named Demetrius, a silversmith, which made silver shrines for Diana, brought no small gain unto the craftsmen; 25) Whom he called together with the workmen his men, together with others employed in related trades, and addressed them as follows. "Gentlemen, this business is our income. 26) As you know so well from what you've seen and heard, this man Paul has persuaded many, many people that handmade gods aren't gods at all. As a result, our sales volume is going down! And this trend is evident not only here in Ephesus, but throughout the entire province! 27) Of course, I am not only talking about the business aspects of this situation and our loss of income, but also of the possibility that the temple of the great goddess of Diana will lose its influence, and that Diana-- this magnificent goddess worshiped not only throughout this part of Turkey but all around the world-- will be forgotten!" 28) At this their anger boiled and they began shouting, "Great is Diana of the Ephesians!" 29) A crowd began to gather and soon the city was filled with confusion. Everyone rushed to the amphitheater, dragging along Gaius and Aristarchus, Paul's traveling companions, for trial. 30) Paul wanted to go in, but the disciples wouldn't let him. 31) Some of the Roman officers of the province, friends of Paul, also sent a message to him, begging him not to risk his life by entering. 32) Inside, the people were all shouting, some one thing and some another-- everything was in confusion. In fact, most of them didn't even know why they were there. 33) Alexander was spotted among the crowd by some Jews and dragged forward. He motioned for silence and tried to speak. 34) But when the crowd realized he was a Jew, they started shouting again and kept it up for two hours: "Great is Diana of the Ephesians! Great is Diana of the Ephesians!"

What was in his arsenal? I believe the most powerful weapon he possessed would be that of God's love and how God had rescued him from the great deception in his own life. After all he at one time had been an instrument in persecuting the Christians, why they even laid Stephens coat at his feet while they stoned him to still his voice for God.

Acts 7:54-58 (LVG)

54) The Jewish leaders were stung with fury by Stephen's accusations and ground their teeth in RAGE. 55) But Stephen full of the Holy Spirit gazed steadily upward into heaven and saw the glory of God and Jesus standing at God's right hand. 56) And he told them, look: I see heavens opened and Jesus the Messiah standing beside God at his right hand. 57) Then they mobbed him, putting their hands over their ears and drowning OUT HIS VOICE with their shouts, 58) And dragged him out of the city to stone him, the official witnesses - the executioners - took off their coats and laid them at the feet of a young man named Paul.

God truly is looking for voices, voices that will rise up in this hour and cry out for humanity, to break the power of sin that enslaves them through the message of the cross and share of its saving, healing, and delivering power.

God is looking for a company of his children to fulfill the mandate for this earth to reclaim it for righteousness. God is releasing a boldness in this day and hour. No one fights alone, even Paul addressed the Christians in Philippians 1:30 and reminded them, "We are in this fight together." As the day draws closer to the Lord's return the battle will continue to escalate. This is a battle to the end and <u>one side is going to win</u> and <u>we as Christians are on the winning side even though it appears</u> bleak at times.

Revelation 20:10 KJV

[10]*And the devil, who deceived them, was thrown into the lake of burning sulfur, where the beast and the false prophet had been thrown. They will be tormented day and night for ever and ever.*

Remember: Satan's judgment has already been pronounced. His day is coming.

We are to overcome through the blood of the Lamb, that blood that Jesus shed was and still is a tremendous victory for the church. **Jesus overcame the 'evil' one and set the example by patterning himself for us**. God's power flowed through him in fact when he came out of his wilderness experience the word says he came out with power.

Luke 7:1-2, 13-14

1-2) Then Jesus full of the Holy Spirit, left the Jordon River, being urged by the Spirit out into the barren wastelands of Jordon, where

Satan tempted him for forty days. He ate nothing all that time, and was very hungry.
13) When the devil had ended all temptations he left Jesus for a while and went away.
14) Then Jesus returned to Galilee <u>full of the Holy Spirit's power.</u>

God is waiting for a church full of the Holy Spirit's power to stand up and establish righteousness upon the earth.

I just had the privilege of hosting a Women of Warfare Conference for the Lord in Dallas on the weekend of October 30th – 31st. The central "focus" was that this is the "now" time, the karios moment, a shifting of God's people into a new place of authority and power.

In understanding levels of authority and power maybe it will help if one looks at how a politician moves through the ranks of government. He or she may start out as President of the PTA, then run for city council, go on to mayorship and eventually become a governor. This could lead to a senatorial seat and possibly vice-presidency or the office of the president.

Sometimes it is more plain and simple than one realizes. Positions of authority can shift and change and move one into greater spheres of influence in the government of God's hierarchy also.

One of the words of knowledge that Lord gave me for this conference in 2009 was that the church was shifting into new levels of authority and power. This shifting comes with change and change is not always easy yet the grace of God enables us to <u>go through,</u> Breakthrough into new territories we are unfamiliar with and take what rightfully belongs to the Kingdom of God.

As we go through this life as children of God he teaches our hands to war and gives us ammunition for our arsenal to invade and conquer plus the divine strategy to do so.

2 Samuel 22:35 (LVG)

He gives me skill in war and strength to bend a bow of bronze.

Chapter 2

A Call to Arms

God is looking for those who will take their cities for God. God is looking for those who will go into territories and anoint and pray and pull down strongholds in the Spirit. God is looking for those who will fearlessly go forth and declare the word of the Lord and stand for "<u>righteousness</u>".

God is looking for those who will stand for truth in their life refusing to back down even at the cost of friendships and family connections.

2 Corinthians 10:4

"For the weapons or our warfare are not carnal but mighty through God to the pulling down of the strongholds of the enemy."

Even as I wrote the above statement the story of Moses and the children of Israel comes to mind. (Exodus 32:1-24) If you will remember with me Moses is on "top" of the mountain receiving instructions from the Lord. While he is gone the children of Israel go to Aaron to fashion a calf idol for them to worship since they assume Moses, their leader has disappeared. So the story goes and the Lord sends Moses down to them quickly for God's anger against the people was H-O-T. He would have destroyed them all but Moses pleads with the Lord not to do it for the sake of God's name.

Exodus 32:25-29

So Moses, in verse 26 stands at the "entrance" of the camp and shouts: "All of you who are on the Lord's side, come over here and join me," And all the Levites came. (The worshippers of Jehovah) 27) He told them, "Jehovah the God of Israel says, "Get your swords and go back and forth from one end of the camp to the other and kill even your brothers, friends, and neighbors. 28) So they did and about three thousand men died that day. 29) Then Moses told the "Levites", today you have ordained yourselves for the service of the Lord, FOR YOU OBEYED even though it meant killing your own sons and brothers, NOW HE WILL GIVE YOU A GREAT BLESSING.

The point being made here is that your stand for the Lord will "cost" you something, yet your obedience will wield you a "Great Blessing". God is calling those at this "now" time as he stands at the Gate of Righteousness who will draw their swords and pillage the camp of the enemy regardless of the cost. And even though the cost may be great your obedience to the call is going to bring "great blessing" into your life.

Because of what the Levites did in this situation they were "ordained" or commissioned for service for the Lord. What a tremendous blessing, to be commissioned by God and with that commissioning knowing full well the hand of the Lord, the strength of the Lord, the blessing of the Lord would be with them in all they did. Chosen by God for service.

- God is looking for some armed and dangerous people who will wield the sword of truth for kingdom purpose.

- God is looking for those who will get in their prayer closet and seek God for direction and strategy.

- God is looking for those who will persevere when in the natural things don't seem to be happening.

- This reminds me of Noah who was a preacher of righteousness who built an ark over a 120 year span in a territory where no rain had ever been seen. Noah was obedient and worked on a project God gave him waiting for when this ark would be put to use. I call that perseverance in the face of adversity. Whether people scoffed at him or not we know Satan must have pummeled him with doubt as he does with anyone intent on following the will of God when things don't always make sense.

How about you, has God ever placed something on your heart to do and it seemed ridiculous or you felt unequal to the task or it even seemed impossible? God is looking. God is looking for those people of warfare who will contend with the enemy, contend for their cities, their nation, and the world. God needs people who are not afraid to get in the "ring", who have been trained for such a time as this.

This is the "now" time. This is a call to "action". God wants to pour His Spirit out upon you for the days ahead. A new mantle for warfare is being released; will you accept the "challenge" at the gates? God is going to increase what He has given you and take you to another level of glory and saturate you with His presence. A new fresh impartation is coming your way. Pick up your sword.

I remember when Bob Larson was here in the Dallas area a few short years ago. At this particular meeting he called those of us here in Dallas involved in deliverance to come up for prayer for an "increase" in our anointing for deliverance.

I had been ministering in deliverance for many years in great power. (Remember: <u>The Lord's mighty power working within me</u>) When Bob anointed me and prayed for an increase the increase came, there was definitely an impartation, a release of glory on my life.

For us to take our cities, our nation, our nations for God we need the glory, a fresh impartation where we will see miracles happen. I had been given a sword, but a new larger sword was given me.

Here is my prayer for you:

Father God, in the name of Jesus Christ, the name above all names, I release a new and fresh impartation of your glory upon those desiring to be used of you in establishing righteousness back upon the earth. I pray for you to release your mighty power upon them and an increase in their warring capabilities. I thank you Lord for saturating them with your presence and increasing the boldness in their lives. Thank you Lord for shifting them into new places, new realms of authority. You Lord are a mighty God and I declare all this to come to pass in Jesus Name. Amen.

Song: I will arise and go forth in the name of the Lord of Hosts for he has conquered every foe, by his name by his name

I will declare He is the Lord
I will trust and not be afraid
I will arise and go forth by His name

Chapter 3

Under the Radar

O ne must remember to "put on" the full armor of God everyday. For your adversary, the devil, prowls around as a roaring lion seeking whom he may devour (1 Peter 5:8). Do you remember the story of Nehemiah when Nehemiah and the children of Israel were rebuilding the wall of Jerusalem? Nehemiah at the time is the king's cupbearer. (Nehemiah 1:11) He is grief stricken over the city of Jerusalem and takes opportunity to approach the king after receiving "strategy" from the Lord to rebuild the wall of Jerusalem and repair the gates. Nehemiah gains favor with the king (Nehemiah 2:5-6) and is sent with letters (Nehemiah 2:7-8) to allow him through territories on his way to Judah to work under the radar. And I love this part, Nehemiah went in under the radar. Sanbalet and Tobiah who were government officials were upset about his wanting to help Israel but Nehemiah did not tell a soul about his plans. This is called "strategy". Nehemiah did not want a lot of fanfare and there are times when God is using us for undercover work we do not want to draw the fire of the enemy if we can prevent it.

I love the fact that Nehemiah stole out in the night with a few other men to survey the situation.

Nehemiah 2:11-16

11) Three days after my arrival at Jerusalem I stole out during the night, taking only a few men with me; I hadn't told a soul about the plans for Jerusalem which God had put into my heart.

There is something to be said about undercover work. There are those that God will use to draw the fire away from you. Some are called to the forefront with tremendous ministries with a lot of notoriety along with that. But, there are just as many working under cover crossing enemy lines and spying out the situation so as to attack through warfare.

I remember years ago while teaching an adult Sunday school class one of the young men in my class came up to me one Sunday and said, "Joan, you're a Pathfinder." I said, "What is that?" and he proceeded to explain. I then asked him to write it down on a piece of paper for me and I will share with you exactly what he said:

Pathfinders are a special forces unit in the army, whose job it is to go behind enemy lines and secure landing zones for helicopters and drop zones for airborne troop operations, as well as air strips. Their job is quite dangerous and requires stamina, and continual alertness, as they do their jobs in enemy territory. They do long range reconicense which they literally sneak around in enemy territory gathering information about the enemy and its movements etc. This way they will be able to choose an adequate locate for an LZ, DZ, or air strip. Their overall purpose is to allow entrance behind enemy lines to ground troops or supply aircraft. In short, the Pathfinder creates a way to infiltrate an enemy's defensive posture and thereby attacking the enemy from within their own territory. Thanks Andrew. I have carried this with me for years.

Maybe this is you. You know in our world today pride has caused many to want to be in the spot light. Unfortunately, many enter the ministry with this type of thinking in their mind. But, let this encourage you. When you are a warrior, and a fierce contender at that there are many things you can do under the radar that many with notoriety may not be able to do without drawing attention to themselves and thereby diverting many distractions that would keep you from doing your job.

Several years ago the Lord added a new facet to the ministry he gave me which is rather exciting. I am all about the war and all about prayer and bringing freedom to the bound and setting captives free through the power of Jesus name. Well, God instructed me to go into different territories at home and abroad to pray over cities to pull the strongholds down. And this is exactly what I have done in obedience to that shift. I remember two particular places that my assistant and I went to where the strongholds are evil and very powerful (One here in the States and one over in Europe). This particular one here in the States was quite amusing. We had landed and took our ride to the hotel and proceeded to tour the city during the day time and praying during the night time. We always do our homework on the territory and its history so we know what we are going into. We were in this particular city three days and on the second night of prayer the Lord told us the enemy is all stirred up and looking for you and can't find you. The enemy's radar was on but we had come in under it and we were tucked in a corner room of this very lavish hotel. In fact, the Lord reminded me that night of his word in Psalm 91:1

Psalm 91:1

He that dwelleth in the secret place of the Most High shall abide under the shadow of the Almighty.

You see that "secret" place is a place of intimacy with Jesus where it's just you and Him and no one else may enter, let alone find you. What an amazing place to be. Serving the Lord is adventurous and exciting. So many times when I see Christians or those who are not Christians think or say that a life serving the Lord is boring, I want to say: "Are you kidding me?" It doesn't have to be if you are not afraid to get in the mix of things.

Well, as a result of this particular three days through our prayers and of course aligning ourselves with the prayers of God's people for this city and territory after that particular weekend a terrorist plot was exposed and the perpetrators arrested. Coincidence? There is no Hebrew word for coincidence.

Remember: **Psalm 37:23 KJV**

[23]*The steps of a good man are ordered by the LORD: and he delighteth in his way.*

We had gone on a divine assignment being obedient to the call and God moved on our behalf of our prayers, and the prayers of others. <u>God is looking for those armed and dangerous individuals,</u> who will take up the call and go into enemy territory under the radar and do some damage, establishing righteousness upon the earth. One must remember that we are administrators of God's purpose. Prayer moves the hands of the one that created the world. The book of Daniel shows us that. An angel is sent to Daniel on behalf of the prayer petitions he is sending to God.

Daniel 10:12 KJV

[12]*Then said he unto me, Fear not, Daniel: for from the <u>first day</u> that thou didst set thine heart to understand, and to chasten thyself before thy God, <u>thy words were heard</u>, and I am come for thy words.*

Chapter 4

Strap It On

Well, in continuing with the story of Nehemiah the work did begin in rebuilding the walls and repairing the gates. Was there adversity? You bet there was. Sanballet and Tobiah were beside themselves with anger at the work Nehemiah and the children of Israel were doing. When God's people get "united" in their efforts, tremendous things begin to happen. But, the adversity will also heat up. I mean the gates were rebuilt, the doors were being hung, everything was being secured (Nehemiah 3) and Satan hated it. Anytime God's people get together and begin to do a great work for the Lord, Satan is going to show up to stop it, abort it, kill it, whatever he can do, he will do it so his work of evil will not be destroyed and continue to wreak a path of havoc.

Everything Sanballet and Tobiah could think of to throw at them and thwart the progress of Nehemiah and the Jewish people they did. (Nehemiah 4) They threw insults, raged at the people, mocked and laughed at them and on top of that their friends and army officials joined in the ranks. This is where spiritual fortitude and stamina come in. Many times the harder the enemy rages against us the more we need to press in to the situation that we are about. It went so far that when half the wall was completed (Nehemiah 4:6) that Sanballet, Tobiah, the Ariabians, Ammonites, and Ashdodites became furious. Now, more have joined their ranks and now they are plotting to lead an army against Jerusalem and bring about riots and confusion. Ever felt like you are doing everything God has called you to do and all hell breaks loose and now you feel surrounded with no way out!

After this past conference that God had called my husband and I to hold and that we had planned and worked on for six months all hell broke loose the week following this powerful time with the Lord. We had already dealt with some pretty heavy blows leading up to it but the enemy was furious with the aftermath. It wasn't a huge numbers conference but the power of God was awesome and electric and a lot of damage was done to the enemy's kingdom. Many reports are coming in of the powerful changes and break throughs in the lives of those that attended. Note: We had done a lot of territorial warfare before the conference along with a 40 day fast, the prayer team and myself.

Well, the heaviness or oppression I could feel the Monday after the conference continued to get worse. By Saturday, I could not get out of bed. It had been a powerful month in the Dallas area as many conferences and gatherings had come in and the spiritual atmosphere was charged with God's presence. T.D. Jakes had a conference that month for women, Reinhardt Bonke had come in for a few power packed days, another prophet in the area had just had a conference and Cindy Jacobs was holding a prayer meeting the night of October 31st which was also the second night of our conference. I get excited just thinking about it as I write. In fact, I received a call while writing this chapter from a young woman I had started up a friendship with through counseling her just before the conference started. She shared with me after I had spoke about the Beatles and their influence in America and what had transpired as a result of their presence in the music industry that she had gone home and burned all her t-shirts, Cds and even old records she had of them. Now folks, that is all a tremendous victory for the Lord and nobody told her to do that. I made no mention of such action I just presented the facts and the Lord did the rest. She told me she had been a huge Beatles fan and I knew a Breakthrough had come in her life. This young woman shared with me upon our first meeting that she felt called to youth ministry. How much more of a warrior she will become, because now through obedience to the Lord she will be blessed by taking such action and none of that will now influence her or those she touches. Don't you love how God's touch sets one free. She strapped on the sword of truth and went through the camp and took the enemy out.

Well, the day following the conference was wonderful; we knew God had done a tremendous work and that more results were to come in the days ahead. My mom stayed over a couple of days with me and I knew that there would be some demonic fall out, but it always seems to be on a scale of fierceness I am not aware of but the Lord always prevails in the midst of it.

I began to feel a weighty oppression on the Saturday going into the evening service and knew I was really tired but would not let myself go there. All the month of planning, the prayer, the warfare, the fasting I thought were trying to catch up with me and I had one more service to hold which I knew would be powerful! I thought, "Oh, my body is trying to go through the "let down" and it is not time yet. On Monday I could feel the "weight" of fatigue, but mom was here and I wanted to enjoy our time together. On Thursday when we took her to go home I did not feel well and the weight against me and upon me was increasing. By Thursday night I just wanted to go to bed, as by now I am not feeling well. Friday was not a good day and I didn't want to do anything. Praying was difficult and reading my bible was an effort and things were closing in on me. I was still putting on the full armor every morning, praying for wisdom, direction, and discernment, pleading the blood of Jesus over my family, the work of the conference and binding my will and my heart to the heart of God. I knew I was being demonically oppressed and by Saturday it was full blown. I stayed in my room all day and the minions of hell tormented me all day long and I began thinking "maybe I missed it. 'No surely this was all God's plan. I know there's a God and his word is true.' Things got heavier and heavier and all appeared bleak. I tried to pray, it was so hard, I tried to worship, it was so hard, I tried to pull something to read to encourage myself, that was so hard. I was in a raging war. My assistant had called, (I had my phone off) to check on me and I didn't want to talk or return her phone call. I knew she was praying, but I also knew I wasn't feeling the same intensity of prayer as I did before the conference from those praying for me. (You can feel it when the covering of prayer begins to lift). Saturday night I got into the tub and was just sitting there thinking, "Okay, enough of this." I began to pray softly and then very matter of fact said, "I rebuke you depression." Before I spoke the last consonant of depression our electricity went out and I was in total blackness. {This is how I felt anyway.} I thought, "Okay, this is no coincidence, something is up." My husband came back to check on me and got a flashlight and we lit a candle for some light. There was darkness over the whole complex and then over another apartment complex right next door. I knew the enemy was on a rampage. The Holy Spirit had quickened me earlier that night about one of the books I had been reading called, "Tortured For Christ". He began to draw a correlation from that book concerning me that every time I speak the enemy comes to throw me to the torturers to try and intimidate me to shut up. This has happened for as long as I have taught on warfare and deliverance and the Power of the Cross and Jesus' name. I drew some encouragement from that and felt an inkling of hope begin to grow. I knew the electricity wouldn't be off for long which it wasn't and went on to bed later that night. Sunday morning things were still rough and

I couldn't even pull myself out of bed to go to church. I had no interest in going and I pulled the covers up higher. By two o'clock in the afternoon the Spirit of the Lord told me, "You're fighting the spirit of Anti-Christ that has been loosed against you." Of course, it made sense. I called my assistant and told her to pray. I didn't tell her what I was in war with but just to pray. She said, "I've been praying and will do more." By Sunday night the Breakthrough came and I was back to my old fiery self. How I rejoiced that the battle of darkness was over, because it was so fierce. On Monday night is when I meet with my prayer team. Tracy (my assistant) had picked me up and I began to ask her some questions about when she prayed, did she call some others to pray and how she prayed. The one interesting thing she told me on our way to prayer night, and I had completely forgotten about this, was that she had been reading the last couple of months a book called, "Overcoming the Anti-Christ Spirit". Oh, how I love the way the Lord works because you have got to have something in you to war with when the enemy comes against you on every side. You always have to have the armor of God on, and the sword of the Spirit strapped to your side when the enemy rages against you.

Nehemiah and the children of Israel are a perfect example of this. Not only did they contend with all the enemies coming against them and threatening them constantly with shutting them down but the complaining within their own ranks started up.

Nehemiah 4:10

Then some of the leaders began complaining that the workmen were becoming tired; and there was <u>so much rubble to be removed</u> *that we could never get it done ourselves.*

Discouragement was now coming against them to get them to quit. Discouragement sat on the wall trying to get them to give up the task, that it was too much for them to handle.

Then on top of that when the workers would go home to spend time with their families in the nearby cities the enemy would try to talk them out of returning to the work on the wall. Oh my, can anybody, any pastor or leader relate to this! Oh, the enemy is fierce in his fight in stopping the work of the Lord, we must remember this always. Well, Nehemiah fixes the problem and here is where we see the need to be on guard against our adversary at all times being aware and discerning of his tactics. Nehemiah in verse 13 "So, I placed "armed" guards from each family in the cleared spaces behind the walls." And then Nehemiah surveys the situation and says to the people in verse 14, "…don't be afraid, remember the Lord who is Great and Glorious; fight for your friends, your families, your homes.

Oh, how this frustrated the enemies plans! They had been exposed, the plot had been revealed, this is the power of God. Oh, don't you love the Lord and all his doings. And, I love this, verse 15 tells us that the work continued on,

Verse 16-23 tells us the crux of this chapter.

Nehemiah 4:16-18

16) From then on, only half worked while the other half stood guard behind them. *17) And the masons and laborers worked with* weapons within easy reach beside them. *{Here it is} 18) Or* with swords belted to their sides *the trumpeter stayed with me to* sound the alarm.

The adversary is real (1 Peter 5:8) and he hates the people of God who do the work of the Lord. We are in a fight and you need to strap on your sword and fight in the day of battle. Do not take a passive stand or leave it to another to do. For if you help another in their day of trouble, when your day of trouble comes you will have those who will fight for you.

Interesting Story (on the sword) keeping it close by.

On January 18th, 2010 I was asleep around 3:00 a.m. I was dreaming, and it had been a rough weekend of warfare. This was Monday and I had been warring since Friday. In my dream I saw someone open the bedroom door to where I was and step in. I remember getting out of bed and picking up my sword which was lying on the desk which is literally to the right of me. I came around the foot of the bed and reached out with my left hand to grab the intruder. I felt a left breast in my hand and commanded the intruder to tell me its name. (Very strange but an identifying characteristic) It was 5'10", a statue of a woman. It offered no resistance. I had in the meantime began attacking it with my sword, blow after blow till it was on the ground dead. When I awoke that morning, I knew it was the demon Ashtaroth, or from its rankings. And I will tell you why; I had been warring against this spirit the day before along with its co-horts Baal, Jezebel, and Ahab. And God had given this into my hand.

Asherah or Ashtaroth or Ishter are just a few of the names this demon goes by. Asherah is a Semitic female deity known as the mother goddess. This false goddess is the female co-hort to Baal. If you have ever been to a local garden center you have probably seen one of the symbols of both Baal and Asherah. They are usually represented by the sun (Baal) and moon (Asherah). Other symbols of Asherah include a wooden pole, the "Lady Liberty" statue in the harbor of New York City. There is also evidence from archaeological digs that a clay figurine (pillar figurines) of a <u>naked woman with a large</u> breast was worshipped as Asherah. I know I had had a tremendous victory against this demon and my "sword" was right next to me, within easy reach. The sword being the word of God which is <u>quick</u> and <u>powerful</u>! Of course this was not my first battle against the unseen forces of hell. But, I was prepared and ready to wield my sword at all times from the years of training and warring in the spirit and the victory was mine. It was violent, not a peaceful take down.

Matthew 11:12 KJV

[12] *And from the days of John the Baptist until now the kingdom of heaven suffereth violence, and the violent take it by force.*

One cannot be passive for your adversary Satan is serious about taking you out! <u>Strap on your sword</u> and take him out!

Song: He's under my feet
He's under my feet
Satan is under my feet

CHAPTER 5

UNITED WE STAND

*W*hat power there is in unity. When I dealt with that anti- Christ spirit after the conference I thought to myself, "Lord, I know who I am in you and the warring heart you have given me." But if I and your other warriors are engaged with the minions of anti-Christ who attack us what is it going to be like for those left after the Church is raptured and they have to deal with this upon the earth? And I also came to realize as the coming of the Lord is drawing so close and the battle has so heated up how important that verse is, "Forsake not the assembly of yourselves, even more so as you see that day approaching."

Hebrews 10:25 KJV

25 Not forsaking the assembling of ourselves together, as the manner of some is; but exhorting one another: and so much the more, as ye see the day approaching.

Oh, how we need each other in the body of Christ. And, oh the power that comes when the body of Christ is in unity. I remember a couple of years ago in a particular dream I had, a baby was left at our front door. I picked the baby up and was going to change it and give it a bath when I noticed it was in very bad shape and physically deformed. The baby's head was too large for its body and on some kind of life support with wires everywhere. And secondly, the baby's legs were backwards with its feet pointed the other way. I remember thinking is this a picture of the body of Christ? Everything seem to be out of whack, and not in very good shape. The body wanting to go forward but its feet were on backwards and the head TOO BIG! That will preach!

You know there is a five-fold ministry that Christ has given the Church that the "church" has not acknowledged. I have sat in church and listened for years to preachers acknowledging the pastors and teachers and missionaries and all their hard work and sacrifice going on and on patting each other on the back and literally singing each others praises while the two top offices of the five-fold ministry have been totally ignored and left out that being the apostle and the prophet. A couple of years ago the Lord gave me a prophecy about this very thing as I sat in my office at the school of ministry where I was employed. And this is what the Lord said, in a nutshell. "The five-fold ministry is the diagram the Lord gave the church to be built on. Those churches that do not allow the prophet to come forth and speak will not make it. Those that do will be dynamic because when the five-fold ministry is in action, God is in action over their houses. Jesus was a prophet, Jesus was an apostle, Jesus was a pastor, Jesus was a teacher, Jesus was a missionary. Jesus set the pattern yet the church has failed in completely patterning herself after him and some in the five-fold ministry have exalted themselves over another office and wonder why their churches are struggling. It is time for the Body of Christ, the "headship" to get it together so the rest of the body can follow properly.

One of my favorite artists is Bryan Duncan. I have a particularly song of his that I love and have sang in church over the years and it is called: United We Stand. The words go such as this:

United we Stand
Divided we fall
We can live and die together
The same for one and all

It is hard to defeat a "United Front". There is such power in unity as we see in Acts chapter two on the day of Pentecost.

Acts 2:1-4 (KJV)

And when the day of Pentecost was fully come, they were all with one accord in one place. 2 And suddenly there came a sound from heaven as of a rushing mighty wind, and it filled all the house where they were sitting. 3And there appeared unto them cloven tongues like as of fire, and it sat upon each of them. 4 And they were all filled with the Holy Ghost, and began to speak with other tongues, as the Spirit gave them utterance.

Can you imagine if the church gets the diagram of the house right and gets in one accord (unity) and the power of God hits they all will have voices for the Lord and if one goes on to read thousands were added to the church as a result of this. We are going to see this but before we do we are going to have to be "united" across all fronts and facets of the ministry, decreasing that Christ be increased in our lives for the sake of the gospel and kingdom purpose where righteousness will be established upon this earth.

Everybody gets touched and empowered when God's people get It together, all become power houses for God, not just a few. Moses and Aaron were in "unity" as brothers when they went before Pharaoh commanding him to let the children of Israel go. Paul and Silas were in "unity" as they sang praises to God and as a result of that their chains broke and

Breakthrough came. They were not only freed and led to safety even the jailer was led to the Lord. Folks, that is power!!

Abraham said, concerning Lot when their men were fighting in Genesis 13:8, "Close relatives such as we must present a "united" front. Unity is a strong chain, a chord not easily broken. Unity brings the power of God into any situation. A prayer-less church is a powerless church and a church not in "unity" is no match for the devil either.

Discord is Satan's game. Satan knows the seven things that God hates which is mentioned in Proverbs 6:16-19. "For there are six things the Lord hates - no seven:

Haughtiness
Lying
Murdering
Plotting evil
Eagerness to do wrong
A false witness
Sowing discord among the brethren

A house divided against itself cannot stand. We have leaders all over the world over houses of worship that are not only allowing this in their midst but are part of the problem themselves.

I had a young woman come to me after the conference was over and pour her heart out to me about what was happening in their church. The church had already been through quite a bit of devastation because their former business administrator had embezzled millions of dollars from them and they were still reeling from this blow. A new Pastor and his flock had been rushed into leadership and things had been said by the new leadership that they had not followed through on and this young woman who had served for years in ministry no longer had a place. I shared with her one cannot go on hearsay but everything she was saying I had seen happen in many churches and heard from many others over the years in similar situations.

You know it is no wonder so many churches are struggling when they are not living up to what the word says. I would not want to be standing in the shoes of many of these Pastors and leaders if they don't get it right before the Lord when they refuse to change and in doing so are damaging the church. "Woe to the shepherd that scatters the sheep."

In the year 2000 the Lord gave me a prophetic word the day before George W. Bush was elected to President. A part of that prophecy goes as such:

"…Many pulpits will be vacated out of fear of the move of God that is coming. The Lord will strike terror into the hearts of priests who have used the pulpit for their own agenda. Many churches will close their doors…"

It is now the year 2010. According to Shiloh Place Ministries posted December 9, 2007:

- 1500 Pastors will leave the ministry permanently in America each year.

- 7000 Churches close each year in America

- 50% of Pastors marriages end in divorce

- 80% of Pastors spend under 15 minutes a day in prayer

- Nearly 40% of Pastors have had an extra-marital affair

- 80% of seminary graduates who enter ministry will leave the ministry within the first five years.

These statistics are staggering yet is the Lord cleaning house? Yes we need to pray for our Pastors and leaders and we need to pray for the "pulpits" of America and the nations abroad.

God will have a house and "His" house will be a house of prayer because the houses of prayer are the ones that are going to discern the heart of the Father and the winds of the Spirit. They will move in sync with the Spirit of God.

Integrity must reign in the houses of God! Unless "Integrity" reigns in the houses of the Lord you will be no match for the devil. Too often we forget in the midst of warfare maybe the battles would be won sooner if we would get all the junk out so God's dwelling among us would remain. The enemy cannot dwell where the power of God is.

Let me add one more thing here, read in Joshua chapters six and seven about Achan who was called the "Troubler" of Israel who brought destruction into the camp of Israel and because of this they were no match for their enemies. In fact until this sin was dealt with in their war against the city of Ai they were not only soundly defeated but had thirty-six casualties. The Lord did not deal lightly with this situation.

When Joshua got on his face before the Lord to seek his face the Lord sternly told him to get up off his face and deal with the sin, the disobedience. And the Lord went further on to say, "They were accursed, or cursed because of this sin. Here it is!

Joshua 7:10-13

10) But the Lord said to Joshua, "Get up of your face!" Israel has sinned and disobeyed my commandment and has taken loot when <u>I said</u> it was not to be taken and they have not only taken it, they have <u>lied</u> about it and hidden it among their belongings. 12) <u>This is why</u> the people of Israel are being defeated. That is why your men are <u>running from their enemies</u> for they are cursed. <u>I will not stay with you</u> any longer unless you completely rid yourselves of this sin. 13) Get up! <u>Tell the people</u>, each of you must undergo purification rites in preparation for tomorrow for the Lord your God of Israel says that someone has stolen from him, and you CANNOT DEFEAT YOUR ENEMIES UNTIL YOU DEAL WITH THEIR SIN.

God is still the same and He does not tolerate willful sin. How many Pastors are allowing sin into the ranks of authority in the church? How many are allowing men and women onto governing boards of the church who are cold and self serving operating in witchcraft, (rebellion) operating in legalism, which is affecting the house of God. How many Pastors are still acknowledging the wealthy to get "their" tithe to fatten their own purses or to build monumental structures so the Pastors can "boast" of what they have done for the Lord while putting their churches in financial straits. How many Pastors are allowing youth leaders in and children's workers in that are former predators or maybe still are predators among the baby lambs. How many youth leaders are using kids in their ministry that are using drugs and sleeping around and the youth in their group that are aware of it feel disillusioned with the Lord because no standards are being set?

This young woman that came to me after the conference shared with me that this new Pastor has a son who is a youth leader who has tattoos and piercing and has said, "There is nothing wrong with that and her little 14 year old daughter is confused about this and other youth are now wanting tattoos and piercings. Are you kidding me? This is an outward display of rebellion. Oh, we can justify our actions but the word says,... "Is the Lord convinced?" One could go on and on how wolves in sheep's clothing have infiltrated the house of the Lord and Pastors and Leaders have lost their discernment or maybe we don't have Pastors in the pulpits, maybe they are hirelings. A good shepherd is going to keep the pastures free of thorns, bristles, and briars (the demonic realm). A hireling doesn't care and makes excuses or calls those who are concerned judgmental or removes them from positions of Leadership because they are "stirring up trouble" or going against the leadership.

Let me warn you of this one thing that I have seen over the years; is that of "CULT" leadership. A good leader will train and equip the church and watch carefully all within his flock. A cult leader will demand that everything be done his or her way and you are touching the anointed if you dare to raise a question. Oh, I've seen that one used a few times. To that I say, "If you're anointed that's one thing but many call anointing what really is a spirit of manipulation, intimidation, and control." Listen up! I believe I could write a whole book on this subject alone, maybe the Lord will allow me to do so.

"UNITED WE STAND, DIVIDED WE FALL"

"How can two walk together except they agree"

We have got to get unequally yoked leadership out and get unity in and then when we war we will have total victory as in the case of Jericho. (Joshua 6) God gave them the victory!

Song:

I got, got the victory

I got the sweet, sweet victory in Jesus yes I do, He is a
    mighty conqueror

In him I will trust all my battle's He'll fight

I got, got the victory I got the sweet, sweet victory in Jesus

for me He died but He rose again on the third day that's why

I have true victory everyday

CHAPTER 6

YOU'RE IN MY SIGHTS

"The eyes of the Lord are upon the righteous and his ears are unto their cry."

Psalm 34:15

The word of God tells us that we are the righteous of God through Christ Jesus. (2 Corinthians 5:21) This is a powerful weapon in warfare to know that as we walk in holiness and purity through the redeeming blood of Jesus that we are never out of the Lord's view, or outside of his reach.

[Song off the Blameless Heart CD: Even in the darkest night and through the toughest fight….He is there right beside me, Always there, right beside me.]

Nahum 1:2-8

*2) God is jealous over those he loves, that is why he takes vengeance on those who hurt them. He furiously destroys their enemies. 3) He is slow in getting angry, **BUT WHEN HE IS AROUSED**, His power is incredible, and he does not easily forgive. He shows His power in the terrors of the cyclone and the raging storms.*

Clouds are billowing dust beneath his feet. 4) At his command the oceans and rivers become dry sand; the lush pastures of Beshan and Carmel fade away, the green forests of Lebanon melt. 5) In his presence mountains quake and hills melt; the earth crumbles and its people are destroyed. 6) Who can stand before an angry God? His fury is like fire; the mountains tumble down before his anger. 7) The Lord is good. When <u>trouble comes, he is the place to go!</u> And he <u>knows everyone who trusts in him!</u> 8) But <u>he sweeps away</u> his enemies with an overwhelming flood! He pursues them all night long.

I remember as I write this that during the year of 2007-2008, which by the way was a glorious year but the warfare and training was intense for me. And through the years of trial and tribulation and warfare it seemed this particular year I heard the Lord constantly say to me, "Joan, do you trust me?" I would reply "Yes, Lord, who else can I trust but you." And all the while it seemed our whole lives were falling apart. Time and time again He would ask me this. It was almost like when he continued to ask Peter, "Peter do you love me?

I know now and I had an idea then that God was going to take Gene and I to a total place of trust in him and I can honestly say my flesh was not comfortable with that but I know him and his word says that "he'll never leave us nor forsake us. It doesn't say that we won't have deep valleys, flooding waters, great fires and huge mountains to overcome but it does say He will be with us through all of it.

[Song: You are awesome in this place mighty God. You are awesome in this place Abba Father…]

Oh, we can preach about the three Hebrew children spoken of in Daniel chapter 3, but when we stand before devastation, it appears it is all over. Not only is the fire blazing that wants to consume us but the king of darkness is raging because we won't bow to him. And then Satan's powerful demons are there to pick us up and throw us in after they have bound us demonically so we feel helpless in the situation. Can we say, "I will not bow to the enemy's tactics of intimidation and Lord I know you can deliver me but if you don't I will always serve you." Talk about warfare!

We know that fire which God was in control of anyway leapt out and consumed those evil soldiers as they threw the three boys in that furnace, but as they went in, bound by the "forces" of darkness there was one, who is the fire that consumes fire, waiting in there for them. The Son of man did not come after they were thrown in the Son of man was there in control. After all He is the one who created the "fire" in the first place and no harm came to those boys. Can you imagine, can you imagine what that must have been like? In the fire, that which bound them fell off, the only thing that saturated those boys was the presence of God. They did not even smell of smoke when the king brought them out, not a hair on their head was cinged. And I can tell you one thing that goes along with the last chapter, those boys were in "unity" when they stood before the enemy and they were a triple braided chord not easily broken.

God not only was there before they were (what a picture of the cross) there, he stayed with them in it and brought them out with great power! So great was this deliverance that the king ordered no one dare speak a word against the God of Shadrach, Meshach, and Abednego and if they did they should be torn limb from limb and their house knocked into a heap of rubble. Daniel 3:28-29. And not only that, these three boys were promoted and they prospered greatly in the land of Babylon. (Daniel 3:30) There comes a promotion, a shift through trust in God when the wars are raging around you and you refuse to bow to the tactics of the enemy. And not only are you shifted into new levels of authority and power but with that comes a transference of wealth. You know what the rest of this chapter of Nahum says, you are going to love it. This is what the Lord does to His enemies.

9) ... He will stop you (His enemies) with one blow; <u>he won't</u> need to strike again. 10) <u>He tosses his enemies into the fire</u> like a tangled mass of thorns. They burst into flames like straw.

Can you praise the Lord for one moment and have a little glory dance before him. This is what God will do to your enemies.

"In what time I am afraid, I will <u>trust in thee</u>." It's not that you might not get a sick feeling in your stomach or a lump in your throat and you may feel your heart might pound out of your chest but know this:

- When you walked into the doctor's office and the bad news was given, Jesus was already there, controlling the whole situation before you came.

- When the foreclosure notice was posted on your front door in spite of everything that you tried to do, Jesus was standing right there as it was taped on.

- When you had to close the doors to your successful business after many years in that community Jesus had gone ahead of you to prepare things for when you got there. And was waiting in the car as you got in to drive away.

You know what the Lord says about this evil king of Ninevah which is a typology of Satan.

Jonah 3:11

11) Who is this king of yours who dares to plot against the Lord? 12) But, the Lord is not afraid of him! "Though he builds his army strong," the Lord declares, "it will vanish."

Oh my beloved, the Lord has set his sights on you but know this, the Lord has the enemy in his sights also.

Song: "Through our God we shall do valiantly, for it is he who will tread down our enemies. We'll sing and shout the victory. Our God reigns!"

Song: Let God arise and his enemies be scattered.
Let God arise and his enemies be scattered.
Let God arise and his enemies be scattered.
Let God, let God arise.

Song: Jesus, Jesus, how I "trust" him, how I've proved him 'or and 'or
Jesus, Jesus, precious Jesus
Oh for grace to trust him more

CHAPTER 7

READY, AIM, FIRE

I love this chapter already before I even write it.
"You are only a boy." How many times has the enemy
taunted you and tried to convince you that you are
powerless against him. That he has taken mightier ones than
you out and you will be like putty in his hands. Well, guess
what? You are not the first one Satan has ever said this to.
Let's go back to a time when the enemy had mustered an army
against the children of Israel and had intimidated them to a
point of where day and night the enemy paraded in front of
them taunting them with a big huge "bully" named Goliath.
(1 Samuel 17) This bully had so much demonic power behind
him and in him that he actually thought no one would dare
challenge him in what he was doing.

1 Samuel 17: 1-10

*1) The Philistines now mustered their army for battle and camped
between Socoh in Judah and Azekah in Ephes-dammim. 2) Saul
countered with a build-up of forces at Elah Valley. 3) So the
Philistines and Israelites faced each other on opposite hills, with
the valley between them. 4) Then Goliath, a <u>Philistine champion
from Gath</u>, came out of the "Philistine rank" to face the forces of*

Israel. He was a giant of a man, measuring over nine feet tall! He wore a bronze helmet, a two hundred coat of mail, bronze leggings, and carried a bronze javelin several inches thick, tipped with a twenty-five pound iron spearhead, and his armor bearer walked ahead of him with a huge shield. 8) He stood and shouted across to the Israelis, "Do you need a whole army to settle this?" I will represent the Philistines, and you choose someone to represent you and we will settle this in single combat! {OATH} 9) If your man is able to kill me, <u>then we will be your slaves</u>! But if I kill him, then you must be our slaves! 10) I defy the armies of Israel! Send me a man who will fight with me!

Little did this giant realize as he appeared that he was coming up against the ruler of this world in the package of a young man named David. Even little firecrackers can take a few fingers off the hand. Oh, how the enemy underestimates those that God sends to be rescuers of those in need. And to be sure, God truly get the glory. One can see why God uses what the world may see as foolish to beat the enemy at his game.

It's no different today in warfare. No matter your social economic status, your color, your age, and your background. God is looking for those scrappy ones that will look defiance in the face in the name of God and bring it down. The story of David and Goliath is truly a story of overcoming in the name of Jesus and taking a stand for the kingdom of righteousness. The Philistines may have their champion from Gath but David was an Israelite champion from God.

1 Samuel 17:32

"Don't worry about a thing" David told them, "I'll take care of this Philistine."

You see David was "Ready", David was in the business of taking care of his father's sheep.

34) But David, persisted (I can do this) "When I am taking care of my father's sheep," he said, "and a lion or a bear comes and grabs a lamb from the flock, 35) I go after it with a <u>club</u> and take the lamb from its mouth. If it turns on me I catch it by the jaw and club it to death. 36) I have done this to both lions and bears and I'll do it to this heathen Philistine too, (why) for he has defied the armies of the living God!

David had been in serious training, fighting off some ferocious predators. And to see one of his lambs or sheep being dragged away in the mouth of a lion looking helpless or being beaten around and mauled by a bear powerless beneath its blows was more than he could take let alone the "Spirit of Mammon" robbing his father of his living. You know we read this story and we think, "Man, that's great! But when you think, really think of facing down a lion or a bear that's pretty scary. And I am sure the first time he faced down a lion after he had lost a few sheep he took a deep breath and said to himself, "I've had enough." And calling upon the God of Israel for his help would not have been outside the realm of possibility. Because he does go on to say in verse 37 "The Lord who saved me from the claws and teeth of the lion, and the bear will save me from this Philistine." You know I remember the early years of my training in spiritual warfare. I use to have these dreams of fighting off bears and lions and alligators and all kinds of creatures of darkness. I can remember in my dreams snapping the jaws of a lion or alligator, or having my hand and arm in the mouth of one of these and banging it up against a wall until it was dead or wrestling a bear until I had the victory. Sometimes, more often than not I would wake up exhausted from the fight in the night. I knew early on I was in a war and the enemy was trying to intimidate me and what I was dealing with in the natural, God was showing me the warfare in the spirit. Year after year I was being trained by God to war, to speak up boldly and take a stand for righteousness, fearless in the face of those that would scoff, or make fun of me, or look at me funny, or spread rumors. I too had this concern for "my Father's sheep". I was tired of the enemy preying upon them and seeing them helpless beneath the blows of Satan or caught in his jaws, because I remembered when I too had been in that position and no one really knew how to fight for me and nice little prayers of "Jesus, help them" just didn't cut it. There were times in my life not unlike now where I needed someone to rebuke the adversary, get violent in the spirit and war for me and with me because I was reeling beneath the blows of Satan and his minions. Because if you will remember with me verse 12 of Ephesians 6 it says:

"For we are not fighting against people made of flesh and blood but against persons without bodies-- the evil rulers of the unseen world, those <u>mighty satanic beings</u> and <u>great evil princes</u> of darkness who rule this world and against <u>huge numbers of wicked spirits</u> in the spirit world." (Satan can take on many forms)

Folks, it is all real and Satan means business and so does God. God has his champions and believe you me they know what they are doing for they have been face to face, toe to toe, with the enemy.

I remember back in the early nineties, Gene and I and our boys had been moved by God from a fellowship we had been attending for 3 years to another one. I had gone through some training at this first fellowship and was being moved on to another arena of warfare to sharpen my skills so to speak. Both fellowships were Pentecostal, I need to interject that. We had dealt with witchcraft in the first one that I was not fully aware of but I was on fire for God from a previous war Gene and I had been in for 2 ½ years. So I was full of gusto because we had a tremendous victory concerning that and no one or nothing could shut me down. After leaving that fellowship going into the next war zone, which I was not even aware of what was to come. God told me I was going up to "Bethel." And this word came in the form of a dream. It took me years to understand what this meant. In other words, like Jacob, I would find my place with God, build my altar, wrestle for my blessing, and never walk the same again. I thought I had dealt with some very evil stuff, which I had but more was to come.

Well, this story is a book in itself and when it comes out, I have always said the title would be, "Not in My Church." And that of course meaning, D-E-N-I-A-L. Anyway, I was dealing with a little psychologist in this particular fellowship whom was creating a lot of havoc in the spirit realm and had done quite a bit of damage to the church and was in or had worked herself into a position of favor with the Pastor and his wife. It did not hurt that her husband held a very prominent job in the corporate world. Anyway, through their workings whether it was intentional or not they had shut down the Pastor's discernment and where the Pastor had once thought a lot of Gene and I a shift had come. We love this Pastor and his family but spiritually he was totally unaware of how the enemy was infiltrating his church. My husband and I were put in places of leadership after a few months of attending and joining the fellowship and stayed in those places till God moved us out. Gene was on the board the whole time and was asked to be over men's ministry. I was teaching the children and moved into having the largest adult Sunday school class. I had been asked to head the women's ministry also. I was in choir, a soloist with the choir, teaching other classes in the church, and working with the youth, helping to plan trips and even asked at one point to be over the worship team music. So, with that being said, we were not pew warmers. We were in it, and actually my whole life in church has been like this. I too could so relate to Jesus when He said, "My Father's house will be my undoing." Church and the Father's business has always been a priority for me and for my husband also. My husband is a preacher's kid. (P.K) His father was an Assemblies of God Pastor and also traveled for years as an Evangelist. His grandparents on his mother's side pioneered Nebraska and South Dakota and were both ordained ministers with the Assemblies of God. His uncles on his father's side were all ordained A/G ministers and a few on his mother's side. His mother and sister both married ministers with the A/G.

Anyway, long story short, strange things were happening. I was dreaming constantly and the Lord was showing me what was going on in the house. The Lord would tell me to look for certain things to happen when I got to church and He told me from the beginning of the 3 ½ years we were there to journal and keep track of everything that went on in this particular "house" the file I have is about 12" thick. So, back to what we wrestled against. There are certain individuals who infiltrate that are aware of what they are doing and some who are so deceived themselves and do not realize they are a pawn in the hands of the "power" behind them. And, some are both aware yet unaware of what's really being done by them and through them. Well, this little psychologist was one of those. And, it was a war keeping her Freudian thinking out of the church. At first when we came to the church she was drawn to me and approached me but I noticed right away the "far away" look in her eyes and that she was caught up in the "mystical" sense. She asked me to lunch and I had her right off the bat as she began to speak. I had already spent some years studying the New Age and the occult and its effects and infiltration into the American churches so I knew the phrasing and buzz words they used.

It is so true when that scripture speaks, "out of the abundance of the heart the mouth speaketh." Her abundance and beliefs were showing themselves yet I did not react so she would not know I had caught her and of course there were no lunches afterwards. She always was trying to get in my space and the Lord told me when she would move in close to talk (get in my face) to step back, not to let her in.

I was dealing with physical issues as this was not the only thing in this house that I was warring against. I had a dream one night and in this dream I was standing in a line with a group of people from this church. I was first in line, from looking back the enemy had singled us out. As I stood there this huge, nine foot tall reptilian creature, standing on its hind legs stood in front of me with this small petite woman at its side. I can remember it blowing its hot breath in my face. I would not look at it and kept my eyes closed. I could feel its strong presence and all I would do is quote <u>God's word</u>. It stayed there for quite some time, I remained still and did not flinch and finally it moved down the line from one to the next. About 5 people down the line I recognized a young man from the church with a tremendous music ministry there, and the son of an A/G Pastor. I will never forget as I saw this reptilian creature open its large mouth bend down and pick this young man up in its jaws. I'll never forget that scene. When I awoke the next morning I knew I was up against something very powerful that was trying to take over this particular house. (It was the spirit of Leviathan) The war was on but I was "ready". I had been trained for such a time as this and I was not backing down. The enemy had threatened me before coming to this church, to back off but with Jesus beside me I told him, "I'll never quit." "<u>For we wrestle not!</u>" (Ephesians 6:12) Satan has a hierarchy. Satan has a government and it consists of principalities, powers, spiritual wickedness in high places and rulers of darkness. It is real and you can deny it till the cows come home but it is not about to go away <u>just yet</u>.

I am sure many in the church are not even aware that the main function of spiritual wickedness in high places mentioned in Ephesians 6 is to wreck havoc and cause considerable misery for the human race. And that they fall under the ranks of the principalities and powers carrying out their orders. And in stating this, these wicked spirits are experts at what they do.

They bring sickness, death, and traffic in the sins of the flesh mentioned in Galatians 5:19-21.

Galatians 5:19-21

19) But when you follow your own evil inclinations your lives will follow these evil results, impure thoughts, eagerness for lustful pleasure, 20) idolatry, spiritism, (encouraging the activity of demons) hatred, and fighting, jealousy and anger, constant effort to get the best for yourselves, complaints and criticisms, the feeling that everyone else is wrong except those in your little group - and there will be <u>wrong doctrine</u>, 21) envy, murder, drunkenness, wild parties, and again all that sort of thing. Let me tell you again as I have before, that anyone living that sort of life will not inherit the kingdom of God.

That's it in a nutshell. Satan hates humanity and even more so Christians and spiritual wickedness or wicked spirits are sent to attack and the main purpose is to fight Christians. Sadly enough today our churches are filled with this. Have you heard enough and are you <u>ready</u> to fight!

David was ready and with Saul's permission (because I am sure he saw the passion and fire in David's eyes) he took on this "Goliath". He was clothed in a spiritual armor more "weighty" than Saul's but less cumbersome. David picked up "5" smooth stones. I want to interject here bringing in the previous mention of the five-fold ministry. It was several years ago when pondering this "fight" between David and Goliath that the Lord told me these "5" stones represented the five-fold ministry in God's hand. And the only way we would take the enemy down who is "bullying" the children of God would be through the unity of these offices working in tandem together. I'll never forget when God gave me this revelation. I was thrilled because the Lord doesn't miss a beat. Then David takes his staff, his rod of strength and his sling which he had come to be so proficient with and steps forward into the ring with Goliath who "appears" more mighty than he.

Here again is a picture of great faith in David laying aside every weight that would so easily beset him, or slow him down, running into the ring by faith to slay this giant.(Hebrews 12:1) Goliath once again hurls his intimidations at David, curses him in the names of his gods, yet not knowing his doom was sealed long ago. For God had one in training that would not only slay the giant but with that would rule as king.

Oh this takes me back to the three Hebrew boys in the last chapter who when coming out of the fire were promoted and prospered greatly. Are you seeing a principal here? That those who dare to take a stand for righteousness God <u>will promote and prosper</u>! Even in 2 Kings 18:7 when Hezekiah destroyed all the shrines of idolatry and followed the Lord closely and obeyed God's commands it says in verse 7 because of that God <u>prospered </u>everything he did! Praise the Lord!

This is the year 2010 for Release and Increase! Again, a wave of boldness, a spirit of boldness is coming upon God's people to speak out for righteousness in the face of adversity and as we do, the houses of God are going prosper, a release comes. Don't you just love it! We need to hear these kinds of things, it so encourages us to fight the good fight of F-A-I-T-H.

Goliath's fear tactics didn't work on David. David had dealt with and worked through fear and he was ready for what God was about to do. David stepped out there with all of heaven's armies behind him and around him. In the physical he may have looked all alone but spiritually there was more with him than there was with the enemy. Always remember this in your wars against the enemy that Satan drew one-third with his tail as he was cast out of heaven that means two-thirds were left. (Revelation 12:4) And I always say, since Satan does not have the power to create and is a created being himself he can't enlarge his demon troops. But, God who is the creator could very possibly of created more angels to take the place of those that rebelled and even more. Does it say this in the scripture? No but since when is anything outside the realm of possibility with God. Over the years of ministering deliverance and seeing many powerful evil demons manifest when God's power and anointing is upon you there has never been any fear. I've had people ask me, "Joan, aren't you afraid when you come up against these things?" I tell them, "No, because Jesus and all of heaven's armies are there to back me up."

God is looking for some armed and dangerous individuals who will answer the call to action, strap on their swords, stand in unity, stand shoulder to shoulder get the enemy in their sights with God's hand upon them and take them out! Are you ready? Will you be a voice?

As Goliath shouted at David, David shouted back. Verse 45

David shouted in reply, "You come to me with a sword and a spear, but I come to you in the name of the Lord of the armies of heaven and of Israel."

Years ago during this particular 3 ½ years at the before mentioned fellowship I held a bible study in my home for several ladies which consisted of 3 or 4 different fellowships. I had been schooling them in warfare along with bible teaching (it all goes together) and said about 2/3 into that time we need to go to the streets. I felt the Lord leading us down to the campus of North Texas around an area called Fry Street. At this particular time there was a lot of demonic activity going on down there and it was quite the hang out for witches and druids. Since 1988 I had prayed on a consistent basis for Denton and had already anointed all the gateways leading into this city and done quite a bit of warfare.

If my memory serves me correctly, "5" of us drove down in my car praying for any opportunity the Lord would give us to share the gospel and also prayer walk this area. As I pulled into one of the parking lots that evening and stepped out of the car the Lord said to me when my left foot touched the ground that the enemy knew we were there. How awesome is that! That is the anointing, the power of God. I knew something was up so I shared this immediately with the prayer team. We all got out and began to walk down to Fry Street praying as we walked. We had walked several blocks when I heard what sounded like beating on a drum. As we walked up the street I saw two young men sitting on the ground just down the way from the local pizza place there called, "The Flying Tomato". Well, this young man was trying to drum up money. As we approached I asked the one banging on a huge empty water jug if I gave him five dollars could I sit and talk with him. He said, "sure" so I sat down. We began to talk and not long into the conversation it was apparent he had a very high I.Q. but equally apparent was his very deep involvement in the occult. Looking back I am sure I opened the conversation asking him about himself and sharing with him why we were there and then the Holy Spirit took over from there. He fired question after question challenging the Lord and the validity of the word of God and the Holy Spirit "fired" right back. [Ready, Aim, Fire] I had studied for so many years about the New Age and the occult and had at that point been working 3 ½ years with a former witch in deliverance so I was not a novice. But I sat amazed cocooned in by the Lord and listened to everything the Lord had to say to this young man through me not missing a beat. I never challenged him, or brow beat him with the word. It all flowed like a river out of me. I even told him that "I" was no match for his intellect (the spirit of it by the way) and he truly sat amazed, you could see it. There was nothing he could say that could intimidate me. It seems at one point the told me his I.Q. was somewhere around 168 to 170, and it showed. But, there was this perfect peace all around me. The evil in him was so very dark yet he looked like any college kid (which he was not) that you would meet on the street. I remember at on point he said, "I'd like to study with you." I remember at the time thinking, "yeah right". What I came to realize toward the end of the conversation of which he did not want to accept Jesus that we were surrounded by a huge crowd of people. I was in the zone and my team began to share with me later as we sat on the sidewalk, young people from ages 15-20 started coming out of the surrounding stores or shops and were listening intently to what was going on. I do remember one of my team standing against the wall to my left in front of me praying in the spirit. I remember two young men laughing and mocking but was so unaffected by it. By the time we were ready to leave I had asked him, if he wanted to accept Jesus. He said, "No". I asked if I could touch him and pray for him he said, "No" to both. I thanked him for his time. I knew he was the leader of whatever darkness possessed him in all these young people lives and that they hung on every word he said. We started walking away, as my team and I and got half way down the block one of the young men from his group shouted, "Satan Rules". I remember I spun around on my heels and it was so the Holy Ghost, I shouted back, "<u>He thinks he rules</u>," and I pointed my hand to the sky and finished with "<u>But God is the one who Rules!</u>" It was powerful, you could of heard a pin drop on those streets after that. It was dead silent. The power of God was all over that place and as we walked away to get to our car not another word from the adversary was heard. I feel the power of God all over me as I write this. This has been maybe 15 or 16 years ago. Oh, how we rejoiced in the car on the way home what we had seen Almighty God do in our midst. It was truly a shot in the arm, a boost for those that went with me that when we go in the name of the Lord, trained for battle taking aim when the opportunity presents itself and firing into the enemies' camp, what God can do. I wonder to this day where this young man is and where those are who listened that night and saw the spirit of truth enter in and slice every argument the enemy had to "pieces". God is looking for some armed and dangerous people! Well, we saw the Lord conquer in that situation as well as David conquered Goliath in the name of the Lord.

46) <u>David fires back</u>! Today, <u>the Lord will conquer you and I will kill you</u> and <u>cut off your head;</u> and then <u>I will give</u> the dead bodies of your men to the birds and wild animals, and the whole world will know that there is a God is Israel. 47) And Israel <u>will learn</u> that God

does not depend on weapons to fulfill his plans, he works without regard to human means! He will give you to us!

And I love this, as Goliath approached David ran to meet him! David was ready. He took that stone out of his shepherd's bag, out of his arsenal and he hurled that stone and it hit Goliath and Goliath fell dead on his face. He did not fall backwards; he fell on his face before Almighty God! Oh, I tell you beloved when you march out in the face of adversity for kingdom purpose in the name of God Almighty, God is going to prevail and powerful giants are going to come down. Are there any giant killers in the family? And David was not finished; he had to follow through on his words. Verse 50-51 tells us since David had no sword of his own but with the power of God all over him he took that giant sword out of the enemy's sheath, took the enemy's weapon and turned it upon him and sliced that giant's head off. And I love this, the Philistines upon seeing this turned and ran. The power of God was all over that place. More than likely if just the tip of the giant's spear weighed 25 pounds. I cannot imagine how much his sword must of weighed, custom made for a giant of his stature. Oh to have been there and seen that. Oh I tell you do not limit nor underestimate the power of God in coming against the giants you face or that we will face in the days ahead for God is getting ready to pour out his Spirit upon all flesh. (Joel 2:28) All, I have to say is get under the spout, get your war mind on and say with me, "Ready, Aim, Fire!" And then watch and see what the Lord will do. Enough of this parading back and forth of the enemy trying to intimidate us. "I will arise, and go forth in the name of the Lord of hosts, for HE HAS CONQUERED every foe, by his name , by his name I will declare, He is the Lord, I will trust and not be afraid I will arise and go forth by his name!"

CHAPTER 8

LOCK AND LOAD

*J*ezebel had done tremendous damage to the children of Israel for she had brought idol worship into their midst. She had done wickedly in the sight of the Lord. She and her family refused to obey the Lord and worshipped Baal instead. And not only were there 450 prophets of Baal but also 400 prophets of Asherah. 14 [Prophet's Dictionary, Dr. Paula Price, Pg. 78 ¶ 4)

These Baal prophets were messengers of the nabi institution of Jeroboam, Jezebel and other promoters of false prophets, meaning they were prophets who served for pay to whom finances were most important.15 [Prophet's Dictionary, Dr. Paula Price, Pg 66 ¶ 1)

The Asherah prophets served the demon god Asherah whose cultic image was an obscene wooden female sex organ, aside from the female breast. She often appeared as a nude woman flanked on the right and left by a lion and a lily. Her association with the lily as a symbol of her sexual grace was to exemplify the "serpents" fertility rites and sadistic sexuality. She was rendered erotically appealing by a serpent wrapped about her representing reproductive powers as a fertility goddess. There is a certain rock group (Aerosmith) that I know of that I happen to see this image on a t-shirt representing their group.

Coincidence? Asherah's cult centered on male prostitution where priests called qedeshim performed or submitted to homosexual rites for worshippers. The word qedeshim means sodomites. Asherah's fertility rituals involved perverse sexual orgies infused with homosexuality, which ended in the massacre of their participants. Are you ready to lock and load yet? Do you see a parallel in the world we live in today? Are you getting a picture or maybe we need to go further because what we are dealing with in America and the world today, there is nothing new under the "Son". Continuing, these bloody sessions destroyed the male worshippers of this religion and were often characterized by mass human sacrifices. Asherah worship, observed as a grisly massacre, allowed the goddess - thought to love "blood gifts" to wade in the blood of those dying in her rituals. (1 Kings 15:13, 2 Kings 21:7, 2 Chronicles 15:1) Same with Masonry. The "Shriner's" hats with the tassels they wear while driving their funny cars, these are red, symbolic of dipping their hats in the blood of Christian martyrs whom they murdered. [Appendix A] She was the goddess of the coast and was known to rule the seas and to take and award the sea's fortune as well. Eventually, she became the wife a Baal. Asherah had her own prophet's staff in 1 Kings 18:19. It was set next to Baal's image of similar nature. Like others in the dark kingdom she goes by many other names such as: Diana – prostitute goddess of the Ephesians. She is also known as Astarte and Anath and imaged as a naked woman riding the beast holding a serpent. In this way, she was known as the holy (dedicated) courtesan of the temple. Venus – goddess of love, Rhea – the Olympian mother of gods, Isi – the moon goddess of India, Isis – Egyptian fertility goddess and is also associated with the secret societies of the Freemasons and the Rosicrucians. Shing-Mao – the mother of China, Holy mother of God – worshipped by Roman Catholics, Madonna, and Queen of Heaven. She has many representations, one being a beautiful woman carrying a child and also that of a pregnant woman.16 [Prophet's Dictionary, Price Pg 67 ¶ 1] Prostitutes and vice dominated her temple worship, where glamorized lust (Does this sound like Hollywood today?) and elevated murder were brought to a ceremonial worship form. Bloody orgies butchered the people, who were <u>mostly males</u>, to satisfy this demon god's insatiable appetite for blood. The most ecstatic of these rituals was the slaughtering and the dismembering of humans and wading in their severed body parts and blood. The priests of the goddess were not above eating the parts that were slaughtered in this manner.

So, with that said, being that Baal and Asherah, these demonic powers work hand in hand against the God of Israel let's take a look at what Baal is all about.17 [Prophet's Dictionary, Dr Paula Price, Pg 77 Paragraph 1] Baal - an ancient Babylonian deity whose worship involved lewdness, bloody orgies, human sacrifice, and ceremonial prostitution. Baal was a constant snare to the Lord's covenant people who resorted to deity worship repeatedly because of its high sensual appeal. The meaning of the word Baal - husband, lord, master - was attached to Yahweh in order to integrate his worship in Judaism. The idea that Yahweh was Israel's husband (Ishi in Hebrew, Hosea 2:16) facilitated this duplicity and eased Baal worship into people's belief systems. The required lewd behaviors, coupled with multiple partner copulation (and partner swapping) left itself to this seduction as the natural desire to fornicate and commit adultery was exploited by the prophets of pagan religions.

Body worship, which goes along with both fertility rites and human sacrifices surround male prostitution (qedeshim) and ritual harlotry. They served the priesthood and engulfed their worshippers with them in perverse ritualistic sex acts. Their ritual ceremonies consisted of gay licentiousness between the sodomites and the worshippers. Baal was believed to impregnate a heifer in order to bring forth his hybrid offspring, the basis for his region, rituals, and ceremonies. A young woman I ministered to for several years had come out of a satanic cult. She shared about one of the ceremonies they did with her. They sewed her inside the belly of a cow and pulled her out through the cow's anus. Sound disgusting? It certainly is but Satan relishes in this type of bestial behavior because he has the heart of a "beast" himself, how else could one explain such horrendous acts of behavior. Its practice encouraged bestiality, which is condemned by God among his worshippers. The custom had much to do with veneration of the sacred cow. The fact that the chief god Baal copulated with the cow gave the cow its exalted status in the eyes of the Baalists. It may also be the inspiration behind such worship today. 1 Kings 14:23, 2 Kings 23:7

I want you to take a moment and reflect on what you just read. The children of Israel were seduced into Baal worship time and time again. It is evident in Exodus chapter 32 and seen throughout the Old Testament.

Between, Hollywood, Rock n' Roll, and their alliances with Washington, America is under siege by the demonic. Baal and Asherah worship has infiltrated every part of television and the movies. From sitcom to reality shows to commercials we have been pummeled in America with demonic ideology. As in the story of Stephen, they stoned him, to silence his voice. The enemy continues to war against those who would speak out and stand up for truth. Satan knows that the truth sets man free. Satan knows those who are anointed to evangelize and preach the gospel, anointed for marketplace ministry and he hates us. Any kind act, any deed of righteousness and Satan's minions are there to disrupt and to thwart thereby shutting it down. Now you can understand why Rock n' Roll artists constantly have groupies hanging around them or maybe we should call them "temple prostitutes" for after all many of those artists are worship leaders for Satan and they have attracted hundreds of thousands of followers from all over the world. Followers that cry when they see them, stirred to fits of emotional frenzy that lift their hands in concert when Rock anthems are being played in the halls of their rented temples, furnished to them by cities all over the world. One can understand now why the free sex and sex orgies and partner swapping that took place at Woodstock 40 years ago persists still today. It's the spirits of Baal and Asherah. Even Engelbert Humperdink, Wayne Newton, and other Las Vegas entertainers of our day still have women exposing their breasts to them or throwing their panties on stage. Not to long ago a movie comedy came out called, "School of Rock". The lead actor whose name is Jack Black called on the "gods of Rock n' Roll" help him school children in a private school setting so they could learn to play Rock n' Roll. Of course, this was all done with a comedic flare to make it look so harmless. When the Clinton's took office in 1992 the song played at the inaugural ball and throughout the campaign was called "Don't Stop Thinking About Tomorrow", they were going to come in and change the face of America which they did with savagery. There is phraseology in the song they used that says, "Yesterday's gone, Yesterday's gone…" They were getting their point across to America that they were coming in and taking over and that's exactly what they did and they did it all because the church was asleep and it was almost to our demise. The Lord stood in direct opposition to them in their defiance of Him, many of us prayed and prayed and tried to warn the church as their dark cloud approached in their running for office in the first place. America better get on her knees in her prayer closet because Satan is relentless in his quest for worship and He is relentless, cold, and calculating in stopping the pure worship of Jehovah God.

Elijah had been sent by God to deal with the wickedness of Ahab and Jezebel. Jezebel had tried to kill all the prophets of God. 1 Kings 18:14, ("Once when Queen Jezebel had tried to kill all of the Lord's prophets.)

The word tells, "Do not let anyone deceive you."

Why did God give us that warning? Because it has been a pattern through time as we know it for Satan to not only seduce God's people into idol worship but to silence the mouths of

<u>truth</u>! And he does that through deception. Jesus said, "I am the way, the truth, and the life, no man comes to the father but by me."

Elijah dealt with these prophets and God sent fire down and consumed them. Did Jezebel stand idly by after he did this? No, she was furious because 450 mouthpieces for Satan were destroyed. Once again as with the three Hebrew children, David, and Goliath and now with Elijah and with the destruction of these Baal prophets, we see, mighty men of God and what they did for God's Kingdom. Oh my beloved, God has a remnant, are you one? Are you ready to lock and load, to set your sights on the enemy while God has you in his sights and do damage to the kingdom of darkness. God wants to and will anoint you to administrate His purpose here upon this earth. He is calling us collectively and corporately to war for the souls of man in our nation and the nations abroad. Let's do this together in Jesus name!

CHAPTER 9

DEADLY SNIPERS: THIS ONE'S FOR YOU!"

I would be less than remiss if as a woman warrior I did not acknowledge two of my favorite female warriors for God, Deborah and Jael. Even though I have this warring nature, there is this great nurturing heart inside of me. I remember in my living room years and years ago it was a cool winter day and I had the fire going in the fireplace. I had been in a time of bible study and prayer and the Lord spoke to me to get down on my knees where the fire would be to my left. As I knelt there in his presence, He said so clearly and plainly, "Today, I lay upon you the mantle of Deborah." I was so excited as God commissioned me that day, knowing Deborah was a mother to Israel, a nurturer in her heart.

Years before, around 1985 as Gene and I were being pummeled by Satan, I had gone to hear this elderly prophetess by the name of Jeanne Wilkerson speak. I sat mesmerized by the power of God on this woman of 72 years, beautiful, petite and full of God's fire. I had never seen anyone move like this in and under the power of God like this in my life. Looking back now I know it was a divine appointment. What we were going through at this time with the loss of a multi-million dollar business that my husband had a small share in, it was more than any 26-year-old woman, mother of two could possibly endure, and I was looking for anything from God to help me cope. I had been born and raised in Pentecost and had a praying mother full of the power of the Holy Ghost.

This woman, this little prophetess moved in a spiritual dimension I had never seen before and I wanted what she had. In fact, I asked God for it. He told me, "It will cost you." I said, "I'm willing to pay the price." I was 26 years old then, I am 53 years old now. I sit here 27 years later and am filled with stories of the power of God in my own life and family and in the lives of many that God has allowed me to impact over the years. And as hard and difficult and deadly the war had been I can say today I would not change a thing. To know what I know has only come as a result of being through what I have been through.

Deborah, this prophetess was one of Israel's greatest judges and led one of the greatest defeats to an enemy that had made life unbearable for the Israelis for 20 years. Deborah was "married" and her husband's name was Lapidoth. She prophesied to Barak in Judges chapter four that God had spoken to her that it was time to take the enemy out and where he would do it. In Judges 4:7

"…the Lord says, "I will draw them to the Kishon River, and you will defeat them there.""

You know there is that place with God where you can receive revelation from Him and He will give you the strategy, time, and place where he will defeat the enemy in your life circumstances. The conference because it is so recent was that place for me and as I felt led to go to my mom's to write this book is another one. I don't write to you from a place of comfort at this time. My husband and I are living by faith at the time of this writing. I have one more month that I can pay rent and most of my bills. We moved back to the Dallas area seven months ago by faith and God's hand has made provision for our living in this cycle as well as He made provision for the conference which we held at the beautiful Omni hotel in Dallas, which was totally miraculous. The ministry God has given me as one prophet described, "It's never been a ministry of convenience." I have poured out my life for Jesus because He poured out His life for me. I owe a debt I could not pay, He paid a debt He did not owe. I owe everything to Jesus, He owes me nothing.

I have taken great strength from the experiences my brothers and sisters in the Bible have been through and overcame through the power of Almighty God. The day I accepted Jesus was truly a remarkable time for me as a little girl and for a few years I fell into sin as a teenager but upon re-dedicating my life to Him again it was so powerful and He gave me a powerful infilling of the Holy Ghost. I have been scrappy all my life, ready to take a challenge even when fearful if I believed whole-heartedly in what I was doing.

Deborah has set an example for me In many instances of warfare as well as the others I have mentioned in this little book.

When Deborah cried, "Now is the time for action" in verse 14 of Judges 4, I feel totally the same way right now at this moment. God is raising up His handmaidens for such a time as this. Joel 28-29

It's interesting that in verse 29 as God says He will pour his Spirit out that the women are the last ones mentioned. Is there anything to that scripture here that the first shall be last and the last shall be first? Is God getting ready to use his handmaidens at such a time as this? I believe so; I believe many women are going to come to the forefront of ministry helping to usher in the second coming of Christ. Are you ready? This one, this call may be for you! FACT: Did you know that women are better snipers than men? I watched a documentary not too long ago on female snipers in the military and a portion of this documentary focused on women as being better than men because they had a keener eye and were much more patient waiting to get the enemy in their sights.

Barak had a respect for this mighty woman of God. Here he was a commander over Israel's armies but he understood Deborah was a commander or general in the Lord. I shared earlier in the book how the outside package does not matter to God. God looks on the heart. Just read in 1 Samuel how the prophet Samuel kept looking at the outside appearances of Jesse's sons to anoint a king over Israel. The very last one brought in before him was this boy with a ruddy complexion and God says, "He's the one." You may be one that God is calling for such a time as this for you are reading this book, whether you are male or female. God is looking at hearts not gender, stature, or status. Jael, another one of God's warriors took the opportunity in this same passage of scripture to be used by God along with Barak and Deborah to defeat this evil commander Sisera. God led her hand and by her hand Sisera died as she drove a tent peg through his temples while he lay fast asleep. [Jael, "Sisera, this one's for you"] And on that day it says in verse 23 of Judges 4 that God used Israel to subdue King Jabin of Canaan. All working together, each one doing for God with what was given in their hand. What has God put in your hand that you can use to defeat the enemy? Whatever God has given you, use it with all your might. Use the positions of authority he has given you, and he will move you into greater ones if you are faithful. Put on the full armor everyday to withstand the wiles of the enemy and pray all the time. Watch and pray, watch and pray. Be discerning, get in that prayer closet and seek revelation from the Lord. And most of all, "Don't be weary in well doing, for if you faint not, you will receive a harvest of blessing. Check your sights, make sure it is all straight, and remove any obstacles from your field of vision so you can see clearly to take out the enemy. Don't react to evil, stay under the radar and always be ready to lock and load and always remember, "If God be with you, who can be against you?"

Proverbs 28:1b

The children of the Lord are as bold as lions.

Watch this boldness grow in your life, speak up for what is right.

Psalm 15

1) Lord, who may go and find refuge and shelter in your tabernacle upon your holy hill? 2) Anyone who leads a blameless life and is truly sincere, 3)Anyone who refuses to slander others, does not listen to gossip, never harms his neighbor. 4) **Speaks out against sin***, criticizes those committing it, commends the faithful followers of the Lord, keeps a promise even if it ruins him. 5) Does not crush his debtors with high interest rates, and refuses to testify against the innocent despise the bribes offered him –* <u>*such a man shall stand firm forever.*</u>

And never forget psalm 91 and I will write just the first three verses.

Psalm 91:1-3(KJ)

1)He that dwelleth in the secret place of the Most High shall abide under the shadow of the Almighty. 2) I will say of the Lord, He is my refuge and my fortress; my God in him will I trust. 3) Surely he shall deliver thee from the snare of the fowler and from the noisome pestilence.

CHAPTER 10

SPIRITUAL HOUSECLEANING

*T*his is vital to your training as you engage the enemy and get him in your sights. There is no need for needless causalities in the army of the Lord. I made mention of Achan and sin in the camp of Israel in one of the previous chapters. I need to take this a little further for your safety and the safety of your family and others as you share and hopefully engage them to take up this call to arms for Kingdom purposes.

It is vital as you engage the enemy with the power and authority that has been given in Jesus name that your dwelling place be a place of peace and God's presence. And by this I mean your home, your physical dwelling place. If you had a hard time reading this book maybe there are some old mindsets that need to be torn down in your own thinking or maybe there are articles or objects in your home that have no place being in the home of a child of the King, Jesus Christ. With that said, let's take a look at what this spiritual housecleaning is all about.

CHAPTER II

SIN IN THE CAMP

*A*nd the Lord said to Joshua, get thee up, wherefore liest thou upon thy face? "Israel hath sinned and they have also transgressed my covenant which I commanded them: for they have even taken of the **accursed** thing, and have also stolen and dissembled also, and they have put it **even among their own stuff.** Therefore the children of Israel could not stand before their enemies, but turned their backs before their enemies, because they were accursed: neither will I be with you any more, EXCEPT ye destroy the **accursed** things from among you.*

Joshua 7:10-12 KJV

Accursed: 2764 (Hebrew – Chalden) means: Things which should have been utterly destroyed, appointed to utter destruction, a "devoted thing".

What's going on? Why can't I get the victory? My prayers seem to go unanswered... Does God care? Are you suffering from...Needless Casualties?

- Is there a lack of peace in your home?

- Are you suffering from bad dreams or nightmares (being chased…thieves breaking into your home,…)

- Is there on going illness in our family and there is no medical reason for it?

- Do you suffer from insomnia, restlessness, and panic?

- Are you plagued with fear, feelings like you are being watched?

- Do you smell foul odors? (Such as sulfur)

- Is there poltergeist activity in your home?

- Are there any among you that suffer with injury after injury? (physical)

- Are your children uncontrollable no matter what you try to do?

- Does it seem like appliances or the car or mechanical problems seem to persist and there is a continuous drain on your finances?

Then, maybe it's time for…

Spiritual House Cleaning!

What is going on in your home right now? What is the condition that surrounds you? Do you feel the Peace and Presence of God more and more or is your home seemingly filled with sickness, discord, discontentment, anxiety, fear and the like?

We have a responsibility as Christians to know scripture, and to abide by God's commands, and to make wise choices.

In this passage of Joshua, Israel is being defeated because sin is in the camp. The camp had been polluted in direct defiance to God's command. They are now in fear and torment for the enemy had come in. Achan had brought in an "accursed" thing. God had thus removed his protective hand, and they could not stand before their enemies.

Well, you may say, "That was then and this is now." Contrary to some popular beliefs, God does not change. The system he established is perfect, flawless and has been effective and proven through the ages of time. The "idols" or "accursed" things have just taken on other forms.

Today, one would be surprised to see how easily Christians have been deceived. Lack of spiritual knowledge and the application of it, have cost many their peace.

We as the children of God have become lax, desensitized to evil, careless in our walk and ignorant of the enemies' vices. The Peace of God is not present in many homes and we have no one to blame but ourselves. Selah.

The first place to check or begin with is taking an inventory. Ask the Holy Spirit to reveal what may be the cause or source of so many problems and unanswered prayers.

James 1: 5-8 (LVG.)

If you want to know what God wants you to do, ask him, and he will gladly tell you, for he is always ready to give a bountiful supply of wisdom to all who ask him, he will not resent it. But when you ask him, be sure that you really expect him to tell you, for a doubtful mind will be as unsettled as a wave of the sea that is driven and tossed by the wind. And, every decision you then make will be uncertain as you turn first this way, and then that. If you don't ask with faith, don't expect the Lord to give you any solid answer.

We took inventory and others have also, and the product from our obedience and willingness has been nothing but joy, peace, and happiness.

What to look for:

- Jewelry - Southwestern, Indian, crystals (spirits or familiars can be attached to these also this is a New Age belief to bring protection to the wearer) amulets, talismans, charms, fetishes, rosary beads, mantra beads, St. Christopher medal, crucifix, Masonic jewelry, etc.

- Reading Materials - Books that promote: witchcraft, lust, eastern thought (Feng-shui, etc.), adultery, faithlessness, glorification of sin, horoscopes, astrology, pornography, false religion, etc.

- Children's Books – Books that promote: rebellion, self-centeredness, stubbornness, disobedience to parents, idolatry wherein the fictional character takes on the power of God, whereby rendering God a useless figure in the child's mind, (Fairy tales such as; Disney, Mother Goose, Pokemon, Harry Potter, Lord of the Rings series, The Golden Compass, etc.), untruths, sorcery, witchcraft, violence, and hatred. There is so much more.

- Toys - Pokemon, items tied to the use of magical powers (fairies, wands, wizard's hat, etc.) Star Wars (this movie has many references to metaphysical practice and Eastern thought), Barney, Pegasus, unicorns, Troll dolls, Power Rangers, Ninja Turtles, basically any toy that takes power in itself and completely away from God.

- Music - Heavy Metal, Rock N' Roll, New Age mind altering mood music, heavy blues, any music that glamorizes adultery, violence, murder, hatred, fornication, and humanistic thinking, etc., etc., etc.

  Reference: Hell's Bell's – Dangers of Rock N' Roll.

Note: Many of today's artists are totally sold out to Satan. Even in the Christian arena of music one would be ignorant to think that the enemy would not also infiltrate to pollute and poison the minds of our children. You must be careful not to be taken in by the cunning devices of Lucifer, the enemy of God, who is called the Angel of Light.

Question: What reflects God's character in your home? When people come to your home, what is their response?

Every home can have the Peace of God present but you must be sensitive to God's voice and willing to be obedient.

Important Note:

House cleaning, "spiritual" house cleaning, should first and foremost be done out of your love and loyalty to God.

Question: If your neighbor or someone you didn't know harmed you or your child would you keep reminders of that person around? The torment would be so great! Of course, you would rid your home of anything to do with that person.

Too often we forget exactly what Satan is about and what he has done. No one would ever call you radical from ridding yourself of every trace of the person who harmed you or your loved one. But let someone do a spiritual house cleaning and now you are labeled a "fanatic" or maybe accused of being a legalist.

Isn't it time to take a moment and reflect on the parallel here? What do you want? Do you want victory or defeat? It's your choice; no one is going to come and empty your house. Your job is to listen and follow the leading of the Holy Spirit.

Have you had enough defeat and discouragement? Open your Bible and read the story of Joshua in chapters 6, 7, and 8, and how the camp of Israel overcame defeat and discouragement but some drastic steps had to be taken.

Years ago our family had obstacles that we had to overcome and some drastic steps had to be taken. We followed the leading of the Holy Spirit and the change was miraculous. God will bless you for your obedience to his word and his leading. The Lord wants you to live and walk in victory.

Psalm 15

Who may worship in your sanctuary, Lord? Who may enter your presence on your holy hill? Those who lead blameless lives and do what is right, speaking the truth from sincere hearts. Those who refuse to gossip or harm their neighbors or speak evil of their friends. Those who despise flagrant sinners, and honor the faithful followers of the Lord, and keep their promises even when it hurts. Those who lend money without charging interest, and who cannot be bribed to lie about the innocent. Such people will stand firm forever.

Other areas to inventory:

- **Movies** - Movies or videos promoting witchcraft, Satanism, New Age, Occultic and Eastern thought (Star Wars, Star Trek). Violence, sexual promiscuity, nudity, corrupt language, Sci-Fi (Horror).

- **Fraternal organizations** – (Are you a member?) Masonic Lodge, Eagles, Elks, Shriners, Knights of Columbus, KKK, sororities, fraternities, Eastern Star, Rainbow Girls, Demolay, The Orange Men,

The Odd Fellow, The Grange, Skull and Bones, "Secret" organizations with secret rites or passages.

- **Surfing the Internet** - Chat rooms, porn sites, games, etc… Going into unknown territory carelessly.

- **Symbols** – Baal (Sun god) this symbol is frequently found in gardens, on t-shirts, towels, blankets, home décor. Other symbols would include: anarchy symbols, pentagrams, Egyptian ankh, peace symbol (remember the sixties) etc.,

- **Objects** – Bringing accursed objects into your home such as: Fairies, winged objects all used in idol worship, Buddha, Shiva, Gnomes. Crosses that have nothing to do with the cross of Calvary. (Egyptian Ankh, etc.)

Note: Get informed. Go to the library there is so much out there to be careful of. There is plenty of information out there. No one has an excuse! God has used people to avail such materials to us. Also, read the word of God, the greatest resource you have.

- **Games** - Ouija (Witches Board), 8-Ball, Tarot cards, fortune telling, occultic games such as; Bloody Mary, light as a feather, magic, Pokemon, Fantasy role-playing games (i.e. Dungeons & Dragons, Everquest, etc.).

- **Art** - Southwestern symbols, Indian crafts, (Dream Catchers), Greek statues, (gods and goddess, their children etc.) the kokapelli.

- **Posters** - Rock n' Roll groups, images conforming to New Age thought. Unicorns, Sun god, etc.

Deuteronomy 7:5

You must break down the heathen altars, and shatter the obelisks and cut up the shameful images and burn the idols.

This is serious and God means business when He gives a command to, "Come out from among them and be ye separate."

Use Wisdom:

Remove items under the direction of the Holy Spirit, if you ask Him, He will tell you. He is that still small voice after all.

- It's easy to deal with pre-school children and the beginning grades of grammar school. As they get older, you need to share your research with your children, because you have a responsibility to give them the truth.

- Remember, you are the parent, and more than likely you paid for said items. Take a firm stand, God will bless you for it. Ask the Lord to speak to the hearts of your children, or your spouse, should you be the first one to move upon this issue. And always remember gentleness and wisdom are the keys, if you ask God for wisdom he will give it to you.

James 1:5

If you need wisdom, ask our generous God, and He will give it to you. He will not rebuke you for asking.

Once your house is rid of objects that Satan has been trafficking in, it is so important to ask for God's forgiveness. You must bind up the darkness and command it to leave once all the accursed things are gone. You have been given authority to bind and loose.

Matthew 18:18

And I tell you this whatever you bind on earth is bound in heaven, and whatever you free on earth will be freed in heaven.

Luke 9:1

Then He called his twelve disciples together, and gave them power and authority over all devils, and to cure diseases.

True story:

I had been called to a home of a young Catholic family with two children. Their little boy was being visited at night by the shadow of a lion. It would show up on his wall and sometimes come sit on his bed. His parents heard walking in the attic and the last straw was when the ironing board walked across the sunroom all by itself. They were scared to death and desperate for help.

A member of my team and myself, with the family following close behind us began to anoint and pray throughout the house (They were scared). We went up into the attic and anointed the rafters. Then we went down into the little boy's room and anointed it. We went out onto the porch where the ironing board made its debut and anointed it. We went outside and anointed the perimeter of the property and the four corners of the house. Some of the objects they had in their home included: Greek paintings of goddesses, winged fairies, the movie "The Lion King", and a few other things that escape my memory now. We bound the enemy and loosed the demonic hold on the family and the house. As we walked through, the father removed these objects as I explained to him the legal right the enemy had to torment and traffic in his house. As we prayed in the kitchen this young couple accepted Jesus Christ into their hearts. Total freedom came to that family on that night and they had no more trouble. They started attending the church that we attended and were very faithful.

(Note: The Lion King is totally New Age. It contains references to witchcraft, and reincarnation ("Circle of Life").

Def. Circle of Life:

Frequent Hindu symbol used to represent, which is the perpetual cycle of birth, death and rebirth from which man is supposedly liberated when he achieves "self-realization."

Cont.

Towards the end, all had been collected without my touch. The father and mother rid their home of it all and as we closed in prayer, they accepted Jesus Christ. No more poltergeist activity occurred after this. The children were fine, the parents happy.

The enemy of our soul means business. The word tells us that, "He is a thief that comes to kill, steal and destroy."

Fads: Be careful of fads. (clothes, etc.) Your children have an identity that God gave them. The enemy is trying to take that away and tag or clothe them in his décor.

1 Thessalonians 5:22

Abstain from all appearance of evil.

Question: What if your spouse has some things and you feel your hands are tied? What if it was a gift from someone close to you?

Gifts are sometimes the most common source of our problem. Through the years, as we rid our home of things, inevitably it would show up as a gift. We have come to a point that this is a pretty good confirmation it was not to be in our home. We saw this happen, time and time again. It almost has become comical over the years.

If there is an item in your home that belongs to a spouse you need to pray. God has an awesome way of working things out and opening doors of communication.

Continual Process:

It is a continual process just like every day is a continual process of keeping our Temple clean and uncluttered with evil.

True story:

My Mom, who is a precious Saint and a true Warrior for God, now 81 years old can attest to that. A few years back my oldest brother moved near my folks. Every evening after the supper dishes were done they would play a game of UNO. They lost sense of what direction the cards were going so many times that my brother decided to fix the problem. One day while he was shopping at Pier One he picked up a figurine that they could turn when playing cards to keep the direction straight. A month or two later it all came out as we talked on the phone one evening.

They started being plagued with everything breaking down, from the washing machine, to the dishwasher, to the floor flooding and then to major sickness.

I asked her if anything had come in the house. She mentioned the figurine, I told her to get it out, repent and send the enemy on his way. Needless to say, all the problems stopped.

Question: Is all the trouble less important than keeping the object? What is the trade off?

Freedom – vs. – Torment, pain, agony.   You choose.

- You dedicated your life to Jesus Christ, didn't you? You love him don't you? You want holiness and God's blessing upon your home, so dedicate your dwelling place to God and keep it holy. <u>Life is so much better!!</u>

"Be not conformed to this world but be transformed by the renewing of your mind." Romans 12:2 KJV

Yoga

"The aim of all yoga is realization of Absolute Brahman. Brahman is referred to as the Supreme Absolute or Pure Consciousness. Yoga believes that the spiritual body is held in bondage by the physical body. Consequently, the positions are intended to manipulate the skeletal and muscle structure in such a way as to release the spiritual body for goal, union with god". 1

Yoga is a spiritually dangerous practice. Many people have told me that they can practice the exercise without the spiritual aspect. But, in fact this is not truth. One cannot be separated from the other. Yoga originates in Eastern philosophy and therefore is designed to expose people to demonic influences. It is an ancient practice that aims to create balance between the body, soul and mind. Yoga by definition should alert Christians to the fact that yoga is NOT a Christian practice. The word Yoga is rooted in the Sanskrit language. The root word is 'yuj' which means "to join". "The meaning of the Sanskrit term: 'a state of union with the Divine; or an experience of oneness with the great Reality'. Yoga means to direct your mind towards god, to realize your oneness with the Divine Consciousness. It implies any effort that the soul may make in its endeavor to attain god. Yoga makes available to you the scientific method for approaching god. All the techniques, which eventually bestow upon the practitioner the experience of Divine Consciousness, could also be designated by the one word 'Yoga'. 2

The positions in Yoga refer to the sequence of exercises that are "scientifically" graded to move from the easy poses to the more complex poses. These poses are to first "cure" the body. Once accomplished, you can move on to more mental and spiritual goals like attaining Brahman. The basis is that the body contains a complex system of channels for divine and cosmic energy. These channels create points of psychic and spiritual energy in the body known to the practitioner as chakras. These chakras are considered focal points or like portals that receive and transmit energies. It is believed that there are seven major chakra points in the body. Again, these points can open you up to the demonic and is a very dangerous practice.

Kundalini is a term you have probably heard of, especially if you have attended a yoga class. Kundalini means coiled, like a snake. It is also known as serpent power. I have dealt with several people that have come for deliverance who participated in such practices. This demon spirit sits at the base of the spine. Once the Kundalini has been awakened it will rise through the chakras of the spine. It slithers up the spine like a snake to be united with Shiva (Hindu god of destruction) at the crown of the head. When the Kundalini rises it produces an altered state of consciousness, as the heart chakra opens. This has been said to be one of the most dangerous practices and not to take its ability to harm for granted.

Yoga is a spiritual practice that is not to be taken as an innocent form of exercise. There is more behind the positions, meditations and breathing techniques than just toning the body. I can't caution you enough on the seriousness of this new age practice. I recently saw where parents are being encouraged to sign up their little children. The enemy loves this because if he can get a stronghold started at an early age, he can cause much damage. Please warn your friends and relatives to stay away from yoga. I have briefly touched on the dangers of this practice. The bottom line is that we are not to bow down to any other god. God is jealous and we are to serve and worship Him only. The good news is that if you have participated in this practice you can repent and Jesus Christ can bring deliverance to you today.

Zen is translated from the Chinese word Chán which derives from the ancient Indian language of Sanskrit, Dhyāna which means "meditation". Zen is accomplished through meditation in hopes to attain an "awakening". Awakening is the goal of Zen. You have probably heard this "awakening" referred to as the path of enlightenment. Enlightenment is about seeing into your nature or self-realization. Zen has its roots in both Buddhism and Taoism and can be seen in the practice of yoga. Through much persistence and devotion, one seeks to become "one" with mind, body, spirit and the universe. Zen has been described as this moment of existence. Concentration techniques, breathing methods and repeating mantras are methods use to seek enlightenment. Zen opposes what the Bible says; we should meditate on the word of God day and night not on our nature or self-realization.

Psalms 1:2

"But his delight is in the law of the LORD, and on his law he meditates day and night."

Zen is nothing more than glorifying or worshiping self. The Bible says that we should have 'no other gods before me'. We are to glorify God and serve Him only.

Exodus 20:3 AKJV

You shall have no other gods before me.

1 Corinthians 6:20

For ye are bought with a price: therefore glorify God in your body, and in your spirit, which are God's.

2 Timothy 3:1-2

This know also, that in the last days perilous times shall come. For men shall be lovers of their own selves, covetous, boasters, proud, blasphemers, disobedient to parents, unthankful, unholy."

We definitely see that we are living in such a time that we see such practices gaining more and more popularity. Second, the Bible tells us that we should be thinking on the things of God. Most importantly, in Zen no one needs salvation, "If I believe that I must achieve my salvation I cannot avoid believing that I must lead others to do the same... Zen tells man that he is free now, that no chain exist which he needs to throw off; he has only the illusion of chains. Man will enjoy his freedom as soon as he ceases to believe that he needs to free himself, as soon as he throws from his shoulders the terrible duty of salvation". 3 All have sinned and fallen short of the Glory of God and because of this, He sent his only begotten son.

John 3:16

For God so loved the world that he gave his only begotten son that whosoever believeth in him shall not parish but have everlasting life.

Mark 8:36

For what does it profit a man to gain the whole world, and forfeit his soul?

1 Timothy 4:8

For bodily exercise profits little: but godliness is profitable to all things, having promise of the life that now is, and of that which is to come.

Psalm 19:14

Let the words of my mouth, and the meditation of my heart, be acceptable in thy sight, O Lord, my strength, and my redeemer.

Philippians 4:8

Finally, brethren, whatsoever things are true, whatsoever things are honest, whatsoever things are just, whatsoever things are pure, whatsoever things are lovely, whatsoever things are of a good report; if there be any virtue, and if there be any praise, think on these things.

Pornography

Mathew 5:27-28

Ye have heard that it was said by them of old time, thou shalt not commit adultery. But I say unto you, that whosoever looketh on a woman to lust after her hath committed adultery with her already in his heart.

MIND CONTROL

<u>**Edgar Cayce** was a mentalist.</u> He could sit in front of an audience and bring everyone under mind control. He believed in Reincarnation. He believed that reincarnation was an evolutionary process by which one could attain the perfection of Christ.

Matthew 24: 4-5

And Jesus answered and said unto them, take heed that no man deceive you, for many shall come in my name, saying, I am Christ; and shall deceive many.

Magic

II Kings 21:6 (Manasseh – King of Judah)

And he sacrificed one of his sons as a burnt offering on a heathen altar. He practiced black magic, and used fortune telling, and tpatronized mediums and wizards. So the Lord was very angry, for Manasseh was an evil man, in God's sight.

TAROT CARDS

Tarot cards are used in divination – a favorite tool of gypsies.

Deutronomy 18:9-12 ESV

When you come into the land that the Lord your God is giving you, you shall not learn to follow the abominable practices of those nations. There shall not be found among you anyone who burns his son or his daughter as an offering, anyone who practices divination or tells fortunes or interprets omens, or a sorcerer or a charmer or a medium or a necromancer or one who inquires of the dead, for whoever does these things is an abomination to the Lord. And because of these abominations the Lord your God is driving them out before you.

REINCARNATION

Hebrews 9:27

And just as it is destined that men die only once, and after that comes judgment.

Star Wars "The Force"

The glorification of Eastern practice of thought, Zen, spirit guides, and dualism.

Daniel 11:37-38

Neither shall he regard the God of his fathers, nor the desire of women, nor regard any god; for he shall magnify himself above all. But in his estate shall he honor the god of forces, and a god whom his fathers knew not shall he honor with gold, and silver, and with precious stones, and pleasant things.

Halloween – Highest Day in Satanism

The traditional practices associated with Halloween are easily identified with the occult. The jack o'lantern came from the notorious tale of a notorious man named Jack, who was turned away from heaven and hell cosigned to roam the earth as a spirit. Jack put a glowing coal into a carved out turnip to light his way through the night. The harbinger (which became known as the pumpkin) symbolized a <u>damned soul.</u> The colors, orange and black, can also be traced to the occult. They were connected with commemorative masses for the dead which were held in November.

Halloween costumes – are taken from the Celtic Druid (witches) idea that ceremonial participants should wear animal heads and animal skins to acquire the strength of the beast they portrayed.

Dunking for apples- Divination. Old practice of divining the future.

Masks- have traditionally been an animistic means of superstitiously warding off evil spirits or changing the personality of the wearer to communicate with the spirit world.4

1 Thessalonians 5:22

Abstain from all appearance of evil.

Obelisk

The word obelisk comes from the Greek obelischos, "pointed pillar". The Egyptian obelisk were quite seriously conceived as phalli.

Deuteronomy 7:5

You must break down the heathen altars, and shatter the obelisks, and cut up the shameful images and burn the idols.

NIKE

- Is the winged goddess of Samothrace

- Is one of the witches goddesses

- Nike's tarot card is number 777

- Nike is part of the Eleusinian Mysteries

- Nike's origin is the island of Samothrace

- Nike, was appealed to, and sacrificed to, for the very purpose of bringing victory to its devotee.

- Phil Knight (Owner of Nike Shoes), purposely named his company after this goddess of Victory, after studying up on Nike's history.5

Question: Do you still think Nike's the best? Think about it.

Deuteronomy 7:26

Do not bring an idol into your home and worship it, for then your doom is sealed. Utterly detest it, for it is a cursed thing.

Book of Mormon (Church of the Latter Day Saints)

"Another testament of Jesus Christ" – **NOT**

Revelation 22:18-19

And I solemnly declare to everyone who reads this book: If anyone adds anything to what is written here God shall add to him the plagues described in this book. And if anyone subtracts any part of these prophecies, God shall take away his share in the Tree of Life, and in the Holy City just described.

2 John 10-11

If anyone comes to teach you and he doesn't believe what Christ taught, don't even invite him into your home. Don't encourage him in any way. If you do you will be a partner with him in his wickedness.

Crystals (Charms promotes healing, protection, good luck etc…)

Holism proponents use crystals to promote health and happiness. A holism advocate claims, "Crystals are an access tool to other planes of awareness. Holism is based on the idea that consciousness can be altered through mediation, visualization, or occult practices. In addition to crystals and music therapy methods include: metaphysical massage, naturopathy, pyramidology, yoga, iridology, reflexology, mediation, trance channeling, bio-feedback, acupuncture and other exotic techniques. 6

[**Note**: *All such holistic theories hinge upon the idea that man is capable of curing his own diseases.*]

Isaiah 53:5

But he was wounded for our transgressions, he was bruised for our iniquities. The chastisement of our peace was upon him, and by His stripes we are healed.

Alcohol

Proverbs 20:1

Wine gives false courage, hard liquor leads to brawls, what fools men are to let it master them, making them reel drunkenly down the street.

[**Note**: Be careful of using alcohol or running to alcohol to "flee" your problems. Alcohol can become an idol altar in your life, taking the place of the Lord who offers us Peace in every situation.

Isaiah 26:3

Thou wilt keep him in perfect peace, whose mind is stayed on thee, because he trust in thee.

Romans 16:20

And the God of Peace shall bruise Satan under your feet shortly. The grace of our Lord Jesus Christ be with you.

Romans 8:6

For to be <u>carnally minded</u> is death, but to be spiritually minded is life and peace.

Ephesians 2:14

For He is our Peace…

John 14:27

Peace, I leave with you, my peace I give unto you, <u>not as the world giveth,</u> give I unto you. <u>Let not your heart be troubled neither let it be afraid.</u>

BAAL

Symbol is often found in gardens, jewelry, towels, and t-shirts.
(Refer to passage in chapter 8 "Lock and Load")

II Kings 21:3-5

He rebuilt the hilltop shrines which his father Hezekiah had destroyed. He built altars for Baal and made a shameful Asherah idol, just as Ahab the King of Israel had done. Heathen altars to the sun god (Baal), moon god, and the gods of the stars were placed even in the temple of the Lord, in the very city and building which the Lord has selected to honor his own name. (Amazing isn't it!)

Martial Arts, TAI-CHI (Moving Meditation)

It may seem innocence enough and appear to be a good outlet for your energetic child or you may feel with a little something under your "belt" you would be a less likely victim of a mugging or some type of assault brought against you but there is a red flag of caution to be thrown up here.

There are in fact actual principles of paganism underlying martial arts. This is an old practice, a centuries old practice that service men from World War II brought home from the pacific. I can remember my first encounter with karate when I was 13 years old when I went with a friend to her father's place of business and they had a place all set up for karate in the company gym. I had never heard of such a thing. And I think that the movie "Billy Jack" in the seventies brought attention to this ancient form of martial arts. Martial arts star Bruce Lee, to whom Kung Fu was more than a physical practice **explored its spiritual depths,** until he met an untimely death, not to mention a mysterious one. David Carradine a well known, deceased Hollywood actor made a career off a television series called Kung Fu stated "When Bruce Lee died, **his spirit went into me, I'm possessed**".7 **Note:** It is interesting to note that a documentary, I watched on Jim Morrison (lead singer for the Doors) mentioned the same type of experience concerning demon possession. While Jim Morrison was driving through the dessert he came upon an accident where several Indians were on the ground dead from the result of injuries. He said, as he watched, he saw the spirits leave the bodies of the Indian men and enter into his own. It was very matter of fact and he was fine with it. Jim Morrison, himself died an untimely death.

Yin-Yang

If you have ever driven down the street and passed a strip mall chances are that you have seen this symbol. Usually, seen on martial art training centers, occult books, new age establishments and so forth this symbol plays an important role in the occult. The Yin Yang is more than a Chinese symbol representing dualities of light and darkness in nature but is also a philosophy. The Yin refers to the feminine (black) and the yang (white) refers to the masculine energies while the outer black circle represents the whole which together they maintain balance in the universe. The philosophy is base in dualism, good vs. evil, light vs. darkness, etc... to balance

 the harmony in the universe. This philosophy is associated with Taoism and began centuries before Christ. [Taoism - the philosophical system evolved by Lao-tzu and Chuang-tzu, advocating a life of complete simplicity and naturalness and of noninterference with the course of natural events, in order to attain a happy existence in harmony with the Tao.]8

The Tao has been translated to mean "The Way" or "The Path" which is the beginning of all things. Like many Eastern religions this concept is not to be grasped through intellect but through living a life of balance to keep harmony in the universe.

As a Christian, we are to look to Jesus Christ who is the author and finisher of our faith. Through His shed blood and resurrection on the cross he made a way for our salvation. We find our hope, peace and life in Him and He changes not. In the Tao there is no absolutes, there are no right or wrongs, no good or bad it is just how thing "appear" to look. To the Taoist, opposites are not really opposite; they just appear that way because of the perception through dualistic conditioning and cannot see how opposites are really part of the whole. Opposites actually contain the essence of each other, and eventually merge with each other. In other words, everything changes. The word of God says in Hebrew that He is the same yesterday, today and forever. He is our firm foundation that we can know that we know that He will not change and we can trust in Him and His word.

Proverbs 14:12

There is a way that seemeth right unto a man but the end thereof is death.

Music

(Be Careful! Be selective, sensor yourself and your children)

Philippians 4:8

Finally brethren, whatsoever things are true, whatsoever things are honest, whatsoever things are just, whatsoever things are pure, things are lovely, whatsoever things are of a good report, if there be any virtue, and if there be any praise, think on these things.

Buddha

Exodus 20:3-4

Thou shalt have no other gods before me. Thou shalt not make unto thee any graven image, or any likeness of anything that is in heaven above or that is in the earth beneath, or that is in the water under the earth.

Cupid

"Erotic god of love"

The plump little infant "cupids" or putti, popularized in Renaissance art were a far cry from the original Latin cupido meaning "lust greedy desire" – from which we derive cupidity. This was a Latin name for the Greek Eros, who also represented lustful desire: that is the erotic spirit behind all sexual union and hence behind the impulse itself. He usually accompanied his mother "Venus" (Greek Aphrodite). The Renaissance painters liked to multiply him into a host of chubby angels surrounding almost any female figure, especially a naked one, or any representation of sexual union. 9

Ezekiel 20:18

But I said unto their children in the wilderness, walk ye not statues of your fathers, neither observe their judgments, <u>nor defile yourselves with their idols.</u>

Feng Shui

The Chinese have used the ancient practice of Feng Shui to create harmonious environments at home and the work place. Feng Shui literally means "wind and water". Its practitioners believe they can alter environmental energies, called ch'i, so these energies flow through the home like a gentle breeze or a rippling brook. 10

1 Timothy 4:7

But refuse profane and old wives fables, and exercise thyself rather unto godliness.

What is Ch'i? – In Chinese' Philosophy Ch'i is the basic flow of energy sustaining all life and embodying the characteristics of the TAO, possessing the dual nature of yin and yang. (Reference Yin, Yang). 11

[Note: The word of God says that Jesus is the way, the truth, and the life.]

John 14:6

"I am the way, the truth, and the life, no man comes to the Father but by me."

John 1:1-4

In the beginning was the word, and the word was with God, and the word was God. The same was in the beginning with God. All things were made by him, and without him was not anything made that was made. In him was life; and the life was the light of men.

Luke 12:34

For where your treasure is, there your heart will be also.

Luke 6:45

"For out of the abundance of the heart the mouth speaketh."

Lewis did not believe in a literal hell and the word teaches the following:

II John 10-11 (LVG)

If anyone comes to teach you and he doesn't believe what Christ taught, don't even invite him into your home. Don't encourage him in any way. If you do you will be a partner with him in his wickedness.

Question: What is your child being taught in the formative years of his or her life? What impressions and images are being stamped upon their minds? If your children are being brought up on a diet of C.S. Lewis what will they hunger for in the years to come? Will they hunger for the truth of God's word which unfortunately is not a daily diet in many Christian homes or a diet of fantasy and fiction and continue to seek more and follow after that.

During the early years of my deliverance ministry, I ministered to a woman for a span of three years that was deeply involved in witchcraft, earth worship, and the New Age. She mixed her practices with Christianity. She was into yoga and meditation and she loved this book called "The Lion, The Witch and The Wardrobe." That was really my first encounter with the book. I found it strange that if his writings are supposed to point to Jesus and the bible why then would she be so comfortable with this book in her home. I knew nothing about the author, his writings, but I can remember being so impressed by the

Holy Spirit that this book needed to be thrown away. After gaining an understanding of the importance of ridding your house of unholy objects, she did a house cleaning. The book was thrown out.

Satan absolutely hates the truth! He hates everything that is holy unto the Lord. He thrives in deceitful tactics and using them on ignorant Christians who don't study the word of God nor have a daily time of prayer and intimacy with Jesus.

Hosea 4:6 (KJV)

"My people are destroyed for lack of knowledge…"

Prayer of Renunciation:

If you have had things in your home that you have now rid yourself of it is really important that you repent of bringing these things in. It is important to ask Jesus to forgive you and pray a cleansing prayer over your house/home.

It truly is amazing how the enemy will come in and occupy, trespass and wreak all kinds of havoc. But once you rid the house, repent and ask the Lord to fill your home with his presence and watch how his peace enters in. So, with that being said here is a prayer of cleansing that you can pray over your home.

Prayer:

Father, I ask in the name of Jesus Christ of Nazareth that you would forgive me for bringing objects into our home that has allowed the enemy to trouble us. I understand that rebellion can enter and open the door to other troubles by things we read, listen to, view, or place in our home that are unholy. I know rebellion is as the sin of witchcraft and I ask that you would forgive me for letting rebellion in. I cast out, cast off and renounce this pollution and the effects of it on myself and my family and our home. Cleanse our home Father, every nook and every cranny. I understand Father that if I confess my sin that you are faithful and just and able to forgive me and cleanse me of all unrighteousness according to 1 John 1:9. I understand according to Matthew 18:18 that as your child that you have given me authority to bind and loose in Jesus name. I understand according to your word that you have given me authority over **all** power of the enemy. So now in the mighty name of Jesus Christ, that name above all names I command all darkness that has troubled our house through accursed things to leave now. I break your hold and loose you from these premises. I resist you in the name of Jesus. The word of God tells me that if I submit myself to God (and I do) that I can then resist the devil and he will flee. I command all darkness to the dry places prepared for it and command it to harm no one as it leaves. I apply the blood of Jesus symbolically over the door to our home. [**Note**: I would take anointing oil and anoint the entry points to your home and even the four corners of your property. Doing this while praying a hedge of protection around your home. This reminds us where the Israelites applied the blood over the door posts of their dwelling places so the destroyer could not enter. ***"When I see the blood I will pass over you and the plaque shall not be upon you to destroy you…" Exodus 12:13***] I bless our home in Jesus name and ask Father for our home to be a place of blessing. Fill our home with your peace, and your presence Lord. I love you Jesus and thank you for all you have done for me.

James 5:16 KJV

"Confess your faults one to another, and pray one for another, that ye may be healed. The effectual fervent prayer of a righteous man availeth much."

CHAPTER 12

SANCTIFICATION

"Being Set Apart"

What is the definition of sanctification?

It is the "process" of God's grace by which the believer is separated from sin and becomes dedicated to God's righteousness. 13

The word sanctified means "set apart".

Once we are saved (born-again) we are a new creation. Old things are passed away and all things become new. We have been washed and cleansed of sin through and by the blood of Jesus Christ.

After we are delivered from sin through salvation the Holy Spirit begins a work in our lives. We have been separated from sin unto salvation. Now we are to walk in holiness. God is holy so now that He is Lord and Master of our lives we too should walk in holiness. (Leviticus 11:44) What is so wonderful is that we have a helper, the Holy Spirit to lead and guide us, to instruct us in the way of holiness.

We have stepped into a new position or posture before God. We are his children, the sheep of his pasture, and his ear is open to our call.

The Lord knows where we've come from and what we've gone through and he has the power now over our lives. God has given us His word, the bible as a guide to help us in our daily living. So now as a new believer as we pray and study the bible we see changes in our lives. Our attitudes and behaviors all begin to change. The old ways through a process are done away with. The Holy Spirit begins to convict of wrong doing, and not only that, we as children of God desire to do those things that are pleasing to the Lord. In many areas of our lives there is no longer a desire to revert back into sin but in some areas there is a process which the Lord takes us through and this is where we appropriate and apply the word of God to our lives to overcome.

As Christians we are daily overcoming sin and temptation and we do this as Jesus did it while he was in the wilderness tempted of Satan. Jesus overcame Satan through the word.

Matthew 4: 1-13 1-11 NLV

Then Jesus was led by the Spirit into the wilderness to be tempted there by the devil. For forty days and forty nights he fasted and became very hungry. During that time the devil came and said to him, "If you are the Son of God, tell these stones to become loaves of bread." But Jesus told him, "No! The Scriptures say, 'People do not live by bread alone, but by every word that comes from the mouth of God. Then the devil took him to the holy city, Jerusalem, to the highest point of the Temple, and said, "If you are the Son of God, jump off! For the Scriptures say, 'He will order his angels to protect you. And they will hold you up with their hands so you won't even hurt your foot on a stone. Jesus responded, "The Scriptures also say,'You must not test the LORD your God. Next the devil took him to the peak of a very high mountain and showed him all the kingdoms of the world and their glory. "I will give it all to you," he said,"if you will kneel down and worship me." "Get out of here, Satan," Jesus told him. "For the Scriptures say,'You must worship the LORD your God and serve only him. Then the devil went away, and angels came and took care of Jesus.

We are a work of creation. As we walk each day we are being conformed into the image of Christ. There is a passage of scripture in God's word where Jesus is washing the disciples feet.

Jesus was doing an illustrated sermon as he did this. The washing of the disciple's feet symbolized sanctification. He was showing that now that we have been cleansed by his blood we still need to be cleansed daily in our walk with him.

1 John 1:8-9 LVG

If we say we have no sin, we are only fooling ourselves, and refusing to accept the truth. But, if we confess our sins to him he can be depended on to forgive us and to cleanse us from every wrong.

Every day we should be checking up on ourselves. We confess our sins daily and this helps us to maintain unbroken communion with God. It's amazing how even little sins can put a wedge between us and the Lord. It's a wonderful thing Jesus has done for us that we can put our shortcomings or sins under the blood of Jesus and get on with our lives.

Did you know that the Priests in the Old Testament who served God in the tabernacle washed their hands and feet of defilement before entering the Tabernacle? This is so symbolic of how we need to be pure in our service to the Lord, also now because of what Jesus did on the cross for us we are believer priests.

We can now boldly approach the throne of God to worship and serve him and make our petitions known.

The greatest privilege we have as children of God is to have direct access into the presence of God. (Hebrews 10:19-22)

We have not only been justified (cleansed) by faith but sanctified so we can offer pure worship and service to the Lord.

Every day we want to serve Jesus with a heart that is prepared to do so. Every day we are going through a process of sanctification so our service to him is pure and without blemish.

Let the Holy Spirit do the work he desires to do in you. Yield yourself to him daily and watch how every day you are being conformed more and more into the image of Christ likeness.

Be holy, for we are commanded to do so. Check up on yourselves and give no place to the devil. Don't let the devil rob you of what God has for you as a believer priest.

God is coming for a church without spot or wrinkle, a "Bride" that is prepared for him. Keep yourself clean, wash your garments daily.

Revelation 16:15 KJV

Behold, I come as a thief. Blessed is he that watcheth and keepeth his garments; lest he walk naked and they see his shame.

Revelation 16:15 LVG

Take note: I will come as unexpectedly as a thief. Blessed are all who are awaiting me, who <u>keep their robes in readiness</u> and will not need to walk naked and ashamed.

CHAPTER 13

CONCLUSION

*I*n closing, Beloved, there is such wealth in the wisdom of God. Solomon asked for wisdom because he knew if he had that he could handle whatever came along. And God honored that request and made him the wisest man that ever lived. Yet in that Solomon still fell into idolatry after all God had given him. Our dependence must be upon the Lord at all times for all things and we must never let our guard down. Stay in the word, test the spirits, make sure everything someone tells you lines up with God's word, and pray, pray, pray.

I pray God's blessings upon you and His strength to be your strength. Go with God and remember: the heavens suffer violence, and the violent take it by force.

(Matthew 11:12)

Joan Harmon

APPENDIX A

http://www.theforbiddenknowledge.com/hardtruth/secret societyindex.htm

*I*n order for a person to become a Shriner, he must not only go through all the degrees of Masonry, make all those blood-curdling oaths, worship gods who are not gods except they are of Satan, but he must make a blood oath of allegiance to Allah as his god and Mohammed as his prophet. The Shriner is then given a red fez with an Islamic sword and crescent jeweled on the front of it. This originates from 7th century Arabia when the Moslems, under the leadership of Mohammed, **slaughtered all Christians** who would not bow down to Allah. Allah, by the way, was not another (generic) name given to God by Mohammed; Allah is the tribal deity --the moon god-- of Mohammed; it was the name of the god in the tribe that Mohammed was born into. That is why every mosque today has a crescent moon on the top of its spire. Now when Mohammed's army of men, out to slaughter all the 'infidels', came to the city of Fez, in Morocco, they found a community of Christians. After killing all the Christians there with their Islamic-style swords, they took their hats (called a fez) and **dipped them in the blood of the Christians**, and wore the fezzes throughout the land glorying in their victory over Christianity. Today Shriner's put on red fezzes (representing the hats dipped in the blood of Christians) with the Islamic sword and crescent showing their allegiance to Allah and Mohammed (and the defeat of Christianity). **Men in Obscene Red Fezzes!**

References

1. Bob Larson, <u>New Book of Cults</u>, P.474, 86-87, © 1982

2. http://www.sivanandaonline.org/graphics/sadhana/YOGA/meaning.html

3. Sohl and Carr,1981, pp. 48-49

4. Bob Larson, <u>New Book of Cults</u>, PP.242-244, ©1982

5. <u>www.Wikipedia.com</u>, Nike goddess

6. Bob Larson, <u>New Book of Cults</u>, PP.299,303, © 1982

7. Re-titled Circle of Iron, it is released in 1987, starring David Carradine, who declares that "when Bruce died, his spirit went into me. I'm possessed"). <u>www.bruce-lee.com/bruce-lee-timeline.html</u>

8. http://www.thefreedictionary.com/**Taoism**

9. Barbara Walker, <u>The Woman's Dictionary of Symbols and Sacred Objects</u>, P.238, © 1988

10. Skye Alexander, <u>Better Homes and Gardens</u>, April 1999, P.90

11. Bob Larson, <u>New Book of Cults</u>, Pp. 86-87, 298-299, © 1982

12. MAY 19, 1990, WORLD MAGAZINE

13. Nelson's Illustrated Bible Dictionary, Pg 948

14. Prophet's Dictionary, Dr. Paula Price, Pg. 78 ¶ 4

15. Prophet's Dictionary, Dr. Paula Price, Pg. 66 ¶ 1

16. Prophet's Dictionary, Dr. Paula Price, Pg. 67 ¶ 1

17. Prophet's Dictionary, Dr. Paula Price, Pg. 77 ¶ 1

18. http://www.theforbidenknowledge.com/hardtruth.secretsocietyindex.htm

Suggested Reading

Disney and the Bible, Perucci Ferraiuolo

Whose Watching the Play Pen?, David Benoit

14 Things Witches Don't Want Parents to Know,
David Benoit

Truth About Angels, Terry Law

Spiritual Warfare, Richard Ing

In the Name of Satan, Bob Larson

New Book of Cults, Bob Larson

Circle of Intrigue, Texe Mars

Hidden Dangers of the Rainbow, Constance Cumby

Witchcraft in the Church, Rick Godwin

Three Battlegrounds, Francis Frangipane

Masonry Beyond the Light, William Schnoebelen

Beautiful Side of Evil, Johanne Michaelson

Pigs in the Parlor, Frank And Eda Mae Hammond

Satan's Underground, Laura Stratford

He Came to Set the Captive's Free, Rebecca Brown

Prepare for War, Rebecca Brown

Unbroken Curse, Rebecca Brown

The Tabernacle, Shadows of the Messiah, David M. Levy